LIFE BEFORE DEATH

LIFE BEFORE DEATH

Prof Dr B B Puri

MD Publications Pvt Ltd
New Delhi
www.mdppl.com

"Views represented in the book are personal views of the author and have no association with the organisations with which the authors are working."

Published by :

MD Publications Pvt Ltd
"MD House", 11, Darya Ganj,
New Delhi - 110 002
Phone : +91-11-4535 5555
E-mail (orders): order@mdppl.com
Website: www.mdppl.com

ISBN: 978-81-7533-314-7

Published and Printed by Mr. Pranav Gupta on behalf of **MD Publications Pvt Ltd** at Times Press, New Delhi.

This Compilation is Dedicated to Lord Shri Krishna

Sanskrit Shloka:

Om ajnana-timirandhasya jnananjana-salakaya
Caksur unmilitam yena tasmai sri-gurave namah

Meaning : "I was born in the darkest ignorance, and my spiritual master opened my eyes with the torch of knowledge. I offer my respectful obeisances unto him.

FOREWORD

Reading the well written book- with the thought provoking title-'Life Before Death' by the well- known Architect Prof Dr B B Puri, one realizes this book is the work of an evolved Master. The distilled wisdom of the ages flows through every line and page. The Blessings of Lord Krishna on the author indicate the Vedic source of wisdom. The appropriate Sanskrit Shlokas together with their English translation help the reader to understand the Creation of the Universe from the power of the sound Mantra 'OHM'.

The four states of matter solid, liquid, air and heat, arising from Solar Energy, and the activity of creation through Mantra, Yantra, and Tantra to evolve the perfect human being is beautifully expressed in this gem of a book.

The genius of Prof Dr B B Puri is his ability to co-relate Vedic theory with modern practicality and apply the ancient principles for the construction of perfectly proportioned architecturally pleasing buildings. By doing this he is helping humanity to lead a healthy life in harmony with Nature. In the words of the English poet Wordsworth "To live and be in tune with Nature and Nature's God".

Prof Dr B B Puri enlightens the reader on the Scientific basis of the Ancient wisdom and the benefit of following these Ancient practices for health. For example in Diagram no. 9.6, he indicates the benefits of exposure to morning sunlight and how each colour of the rainbow affects different Chakras in the Human Aura and in turn controls the body.

His concern with clean air and the problems of air

pollution are part of the environment consciousness of his students and readers.

The main theme of the book is LIVE IN THE PRESENT MOMENT. Do the right thing now at this moment and the future will take care of itself. Right action leads to right results. Following the ancient Vedic wisdom results in Spiritual Evolution and the Creation of the Perfect Man.

As President of Zoroastrian College I consider it a privilege to mention that Prof Dr B B Puri has graciously consented to be a senior Faculty member of our college and head of the vastu department. He conducts education in the true and old Gurukul method.

His students are fortunate to be touched by the grace of such a highly evolved Spiritual Master who at the same time is a versatile practicing Architect, member of many social organizations and founder chairman of several research centres. He is held in high esteem by Presidents and Prime Ministers of India and other distinguished persons in public life.

As his sincere admirer and well wisher I congratulate him on the excellence of this book. May he continue to write many more books for the Universal benefit of humanity.

Dame Dr Prof Meher Master-Moos
President, Zoroastrian College, Mumbai
All India SHAH BEHRAM BAUG SOCIETY (for Scientific & Educational Research); AND MAZDAYASNIE MONASTERIE
D. Sc.; Ph. D.; (Med. Alt) D. D.; D. Litt. (Honoris Causa.). M.A. (Oxon) LLM. (Michigan Ann Arbor):
Of Lincoln's Inn Barrister-at-law; Advocate; Special Executive Magistrate (Maharashtra India)
Vice-Chancellor in charge of the International Legal Affairs of the OIUCM (Sri Lanka);
Representative at the United Nations of SBBS/ Zoroastrian College, an NGO in Special Consultative Status with the United Nations Economic and Social Council.

Letter to Readers

My Dear Readers,

This book is for you. The fact that you are reading this book indicates that you want to live a more fulfilling, peaceful and richer life and enjoy every moment of your LIFE BEFORE DEATH.

May this book guide your life with inspiration, guidance, comfort and wisdom.

This book will help you achieve new goals, develop a better sense and purpose of life, and generate many new ideas about self and your future, guarantee a lifetime of success.

People in general simply accept failures as their fate. A few may succeed by chance or by accident, but most of them suffer through a lifetime of frustration and unhappiness. They have neither the determination to succeed nor the willingness to devote time and effort necessary to achieve success.

This book is not for them, unless they take this book as a guidebook or as a workbook. This book is not meant for gulping the whole book down in one reading. It should be read carefully and understood.

The purpose of this book is to help you in creating an action plan for the rest of your life.

With love and Blessings, in the service of a Healthy Nation.

Prof Dr B B Puri

ACKNOWLEDGEMENT

Whatever I learn from the different religious societies and my experience over the last 50 years, I have tried to share and explain the same in this book. Moreover I have tried to express the true knowledge as I learn and understood from Bhagavad Gita.

I, therefore, have decided to pen down my experiences with the aid of Vedic knowledge. My books are a practical guide to attain *An Ageless Mind,* with the help of the spiritual laws contained in Vedic Knowledge and derive their benefits through the *Art of Blissful Living.*

My grateful acknowledgement is made to my readers, who have given me encouragement to write this book of knowledge.

I wish to express my sincere thanks to my family and friends for the wholehearted support and inspiration given to me in accomplishing this work.

I also thank the publisher MD Publications Pvt Ltd, New Delhi, for bringing out this book. I am also grateful to Mr Pranav Gupta, Director, MD Publications Pvt Ltd, New Delhi, for giving personal attention in the production of this book.

Last, but not the least, I offer my sincere thanks to all my clients, students, staff and faculty, of Vastu Research Centre, Design Gurukul, Zoroastrian College (Mumbai), Board of Trustees of Research Institute of Vedic Culture (RIVC), and World Academy of Spiritual Science (WASS) for their cooperation and full support.

Prof Dr B B Puri

Life and Achievements of Prof Dr B B Puri

Prof Dr B B Puri is a multifaceted personality and he is a Senior Practicing Architect, Research Scholar, Author and Vastu Advisor. He is associated with numerous professional organizations. His achievements highlight his versatile character.

Prof Puri has added a new research dimension and scientific approach to Vedic Culture making it a modern concept. His mission is to propagate the new dimensions in the Vedic Philosophy and get due recognition for it.

Prof Puri's creative ability has earned him many commendations from Dr. Zakir Hussain, Shri V. V. Giri, Dr. Giani Zail Singh, and Dr. Shankar Dayal Sharma, Shri. K. R. Narayanan, Former Presidents of India. He was also honoured with a shield and testimonial by Smt. Indira Gandhi, and Shri. Rajiv Gandhi, Former Prime Ministers of India. He has traveled widely and has participated in and headed many National and International Conferences and Seminars.

He is the recipient of numerous awards and notes of appreciation from renowned personalities. He has been honored with the **Bharat Gaurav Award** (1996), **Bhaskar Award** (1997), **Business Initiative Development Award** (1998), **The Gem of India Award** (1998), **National**

Excellency Award (1999), **Health Excellence Award** (2000), **The International Academician Fellowship Award** (2002). A Biographical note on Prof Puri was featured in **India's Who's Who Book** (1978) and **Prominent Personalities of India**, (1979). **Master of Wisdom National Award** 2008 by Media Trust of India, **Vedic Signature Award** 2008. On 27th May 2009, the M.G.I & R.T.I. Moka Mauritius, awarded **THE LIGHT OF EAST Award 2009** to Prof Dr B B Puri.

He has been honored with **The Millennium Award** and a Gold Medal at the Millennium World Congress (2000) for his lifetime achievements.

Prof Puri has written more than 120 books, the then Hon'ble President of India has released his popular books titled 'Vedic Architecture & Art of Living' and 'Applied Vastu Shastra in Modern Architecture. His latest book titled "Vastu Science For 21st Century to Enjoy the Gift of Nature'. 'The Ageless Mind', 'The Art of Blissful Living, Spiritual laws of Vedic Philosophy' and 'Life Before Death' have been well received.

Present Positions held by Prof Dr B B Puri

President	:	Grover & Puri, Chartered Architects, Engineers & Town Planners (In service's to the Nation, since 1960).
Founder & Vice Chairman	:	Vastu Kala Academy College of Architecture, offers 5 years degree course in Architecture. It is affiliated to the prestigious G.G.S Indraprastha University, New Delhi (Since 1992).
Founder & Chairman	:	The Institution of Vastu Science (India) (A National Council of Vastu Consultants Since 2000).

Founder & Chairman Board of Trustees	:	Research Institute of Vedic Culture. Regd. Trust. N.G.O. (Since 2000.)
Founder & Chairman	:	Vastu Research Centre (Since 1996) Centre deals with teaching, training, workshops, seminars, and research on Vedic Architecture & Vastu Science upto Ph.D. level.
Chairman	:	Vedic Vastu Research Department Zoroastrian College (Since 2003).
Head of occult Science Dept.	:	Zoroastrian College (Mumbai) (Since 2002)
Founder & Chairman	:	Design Gurukul. A pioneer institution for professionals (Since 2006).
Founder & Director	:	World Academy of Spiritual Sciences (WASS) (Since 2005).
Life Member	:	India International Centre (Since 1973).
Life Member	:	Indian council of Social Welfare (Since 1978).
Life Member	:	ISKCON (Since 1980).
Life Member	:	Indian building Congress (Since 1993).
Life Member	:	International Council of Consultants (Since 1995).
Life Member	:	Council of Architecture (Since 1977).
Member	:	Institute of Chartered Engineers (Since1955).
Member	:	India Habitat Centre (Since 1994).
Asso. Member	:	A.M. I.C.E. India & U.S.A (Since1965).
Member	:	Royal Arch Mason (Since 1968).
Member	:	Starling management committee

		ISKCON Kailash Colony New Delhi (Since 2005).
Member	:	Alumnae member ship certificate of the friends of ZOROASTRIAN COLLEGE, conferred in appreciation of Promotion of cultural and scientific & academic Co. operation at convocation ceremony.
Advisor	:	Draupadi Trust. (Since 2006)
Emeritus	:	Professor Zoroastrian College (Mumbai) (2003)

Guidance to Ph D, Research scholars.

Past Positions held by Prof Dr B B Puri

Founder & Vice President	:	War Widows Association (1971-85).
Vice President	:	Indo-French Friendship Association (1974-80).
Chairman Board of Trustee	:	Utthan Charitable Trust (1992-96).
Chairman	:	Vastu Gyan Publication (1998-2000).
Chairman	:	ISE Film & Television (1999-2000).
Chairman	:	Euro- Asia Equitech (India) Ltd (1992-94).
Chairman	:	Grover & Puri International (1989-92).
Chairman	:	Environment Committee Rotary Club. Delhi (1989-90).
Director	:	Prabhupada Institute of Culture (1989-90).

Director	:	Auvitec Techno India Pvt. Ltd (1983-85).
Director	:	Top line Sheeting Pvt. Ltd (1982- 85).
Mng. Director	:	Miralam Lake Resort Pvt. Ltd (1980-84).
Mng. Director	:	Abha Lake Resorts Pvt. Ltd (1980-84).
Director	:	Ahura Estates Pvt. Ltd (1980-85).
Mng. Director	:	Naetzker Thorasell Gostomski Grover & Puri International Indo-American collaboration of Architecture, U.S.A. (1976- 79).
Member	:	Northern Railway Consultative Committee, Govt. of India (1974-76).
Member	:	Indo- German Chamber of Commerce (1973-82).
Member	:	India Federation of UN Association (1973-85).
Member	:	Indo-American Chamber of Commerce (1972-80).
Member	:	Traffic Police Road Safety Committee (1970-75).
Chairman & Mng. Director	:	International Export Private Ltd. (1971-2001).
Chairman & Mng. Director	:	Shringarak Pvt. Ltd (1972-92).
Vice Chairman	:	Theatre Panorama (1975-79).
Chairman	:	Might of India, Trade And Industrial Journal (1972- 74).
Secretary	:	Natya Ballet Centre (1980- 85).
Proprietor	:	Bhushan Bros. (1953-1990).

Some of the Books written By Prof Dr B B Puri

- **Mass Scale Housing for Hot Climate.**
  (Published by Oxford & IBH Publishing Co. Pvt. Ltd. 1993)
- **Vedic Architecture & Art of Living.**
  (Published by Vastu Gyan Publication 1995)
- **Applied Vastu Shastra in Modern Architecture.**
  (Published by Vastu Gyan Publication 1997).
- **Vastu Science for 21st Century, To Enjoy The Gift Of Nature.**
  (Published by New Age Books 2002, 2003 & 2004.)
- **The Role of Vedic Culture to enjoy Beneficial Living**
  (Published by Research Institute of Vedic Culture, 2003)
- **A Practical Guide to an Ageless Mind**
  (Published by Research Institute of Vedic Culture, 2004)
- **The Art of Blissfull Living.**
  (Published by Motilal Banarsidas Publisers Pvt. Ltd 2007)
- **Life Before Death**
  (Published by MD Publications Pvt Ltd, 2010)

Technical Papers written By Prof Dr B B Puri

- Industrial Architecture.
  (Technical Paper Presented at Soviet- Indian Seminar, Moscow, U.S.S.R.) (From 27th Aug. to 1st Sept., 1990)
- Vedic Architecture.
  (Technical Paper Presented at Soviet- Indian Seminar, Moscow, U.S.S.R.) (From 27th Aug. 1st Sept., 1990)
- Modern Architecture.
  (Technical Paper Presented at Soviet- Indian Seminar, Moscow, U.S.S.R.)(From 27th Aug. 1st Sept., 1990)

- Landscape Architecture.
  (Technical Paper Presented at Soviet- Indian Seminar, Moscow, U.S.S.R.) (From 27th Aug &1st Sept., 1990).
- Modular Architecture.
- Shelter in Hot Climate.
- Solar Efficient Building Design.
- Environmental Science (Lighting, Electrical, Mechanical Services).
- Planning & Designing Market Places.
- Economical Problems in Environmental Control.
- Economical of space Planning and Construction.
- Theory for Planning, Design of Group Housing of Large Campuses.
- Low Cost Housing, Planning, Designing, Layout Technique.
- Non- conventional building material suitable for Low Cost Housing.
- Building Science faculty an In-service Course on Landscaping.
- Quality Improvement in Preliminary Construction Material.
- Climatology.
- Dwelling in Different Parts of Climatical Zone.
- New Direction in Architecture Education.
- Cosmic Energy from Air, Light & Color.
- Sunlight for Efficient Building Design.
- Landscaping in Natural Environment.
- Green Buildings.
- Energy from five Elements.
- Solar Efficient Building Design.

AWARDS

YEAR	AWARDS
1996	Bharat Gaurav Award
1996	Bharat Nirman Award
1997	Bhaskar Award
1997	Mystique India Award
1998	Gem Of India Award
1998	Business Initiative Development Award
1999	National Excellency Award
2000	Millennium Award & Gold Medal (Lifetime achievement award) (A Birthday gift on 8th Jan 2000)
2000	Millennium World Congress of Holistic Health Science Award
2002	Silver Jubilee In Appreciation of the Invaluable services Rendered to the cause of Education as a Guest Lecturer and Speaker Award.
2002	Silver Jubilee World Congress of Medicina Alternativa Holistic Health Spiritual Science Award
2002	Health Excellence Award
2002	The Institution of Vastu Science (India) Award
2002-05	Appreciation Award
2003	Conferring the Title (Honoris Causa) of Vedic Vastu Research Head of Department Chairperson
2003	Conferring on Emeritus Professor
2003-04	Aquarian Age World Congress of Medicina Alternativa Holistic Health Spiritual Science Award
2003	Distinguished Academician Award

2004-05	Group Delegation Head Special Award
2003	19th World Congress of Science & Spirituality (Medicina Alternativa) Award
2005	International Fellowship of The Friends of The Zoroastrian College Circle Award
2005	Revival of Vedic Wisdom Award
2007	Peace Award, (21st January 2007) for Truth, Religion Peace, love health and Non valence
2007	Speaker Special Award
2007	Awarded The Title of Head of Board of Studies & Chief Guide for Delhi Region for VRC, by COSMIC HEALING WORLD CONGRESS.
2007	Alumnae Certificate of the Friends of ZOROASTRIAN COLLEGE, conferred in appreciation of Promotions of cultural and scientific & Academic Co-operation at Convocation Ceremony.
2008	Master of Wisdom Award By Media Trust of India
2009	Vedic Signature Award by Media Trust of India
2009	The LIGHT OF EAST Award by M.G.I. Mauritius

Hon'ble President of India, Shri Shankar Dayal Sharma, on 26th December, 1995 at Rashtrapati Bhawan, New Delhi, has released the first edition of the book titled Vedic Architecture and Art of Living written by Prof Dr B B Puri

Shri Zakir Hussain, the President of India, made the above observation, after inspecting the detailed plans prepared by B. B. Puri. Architect, on the eve of laying the foundation stone of S.G.T.B. Khalsa College, Delhi University.

Prof B B Puri along with Russian deligation, discussion with Shri Rajiv Gandhi Former Prime Minister of India

Prof B B Puri with Smt. Shiela Dixit, Chief Minister, New Delhi

Prof Dr B B Puri getting the blessing from
Late Shri V. V. Giri the president of India

Shri V V Giri , President of India,
Presenting Award of Appreciation to Prof Puri

Prof. Puri with Ph.D. Research Scholar students

Prof. Puri awarding Ph.D. Degrees to students

Prof. Puri with Ph.D. Research Scholar students

Prof. Puri awarding Degree to Ph.D.students

AWARDS AND HONOURS

Dr. Puri with President & Prime Minister of India

PROF. PURI WITH VIP'S

Books Released by V.V.I.P. Authored by Prof. Dr. B. B. Puri

Prof. Puri Presenting his book to **Shri. R. K. Narayanan Former President of India.**

Book Released by **Hon'ble President of India, Shri Shankar Dayal Sharma,** on 3'rd July 1997 at Rashtrapati Bhawan.

Released by **Swami Chinmayanand Ji Minister of State** for Home Affairs on 7th April 2003, at India Habitat Centre

Released by **Hon'ble President of India, Shri Shankar Dayal Sharma**, on 26th Dec, 1995 at Rashtrapati Bhawan, New Delhi.

H. E. the Governor of Bihar, releasing "Mass Scale Housing For Hot Climate" A book on architecture authored by Prof. Dr. B. B. Puri

H.E. Consul General Alexander Mantysky Releasing the Book's Author by Prof. Dr. B. B. Puri, at Russia Cultural Centre in Present of Dame Dr. Prof. Meher Master Moos

Prof. B. B. Puri with H.E. Mr. Anirood Jagnauth President Republic of Mauritius on 29th May 2009 at President House Mauritius

Dr. Najma Heptulla, Former Deputy Chairman (Rajya Sabha) and **Dr. Harsh Vardhan**, President Bharatiya Janata Party Delhi. Releasing book titled "The Art of Blissful Living", Authored by Prof. Dr. B. B. Puri.

Release of two book's titled Spiritual laws of Vedic Philosophy & Vastu Science for 21st Century to enjoy the gift of nature (New Edition)" Authored by Prof. Dr. B. B. Puri by **Hon'ble Minister Smt. Ambika Soni**, Minister of Tourism & Culture, Government of India.

Master of Wisdom Award Presented to Prof. Puri by **Media Trust of India**

Vedic Signature (2008) Award Presenting to Prof Puri by **Smt. Ambika Soni, Minister of Tourism & Culture Government of India**

Prof. Puri receiving shield of testimonial from
Late Smt. Indira Gandhi. Prime Minister of India

Contents

Curtain Raiser about the Books written by Prof Dr B B Puri

My previous books titled *Vedic Architecture and Art of Living and Applied Vastu Shastra in Modern Architecture* have been well received by the readers. While releasing the book in a function held at Rashtrapati Bhawan on 26th December 1995, His Excellency, Dr. Shankar Dayal Sharma, The Hon'ble President of India, had all praise for the book. Doordarshan and the print media covered the event extensively.

Earlier, at the presentation Function at Jubilee Hall, Hyderabad, Smt. Vimla Sharma, First Lady of India, presented the book to Smt. Urmila Ben Patel, the then Hon'ble Union Minister for Power in the presence of Smt. Suman Krishna Kant, the First Lady of Andhra Pradesh, Shri Krishna Kant, Hon'ble Governor of Andhra Pradesh, Shri Chandra Babu Naidu, The then Hon'ble Chief Minister of Andhra Pradesh and Shri Mallikarjun, The then Hon'ble Union Minister for Defence and Railways.

While I was working on the third Volume, a number of my students and clients encouraged me to write on the ways and means to attain peace of mind and tranquility.

The overwhelming response and encouragement for my endeavours has prompted me to present you the third Volume on the subject titled *A Practical Guide to an Ageless Mind*.

While man's physical structure has remained unchanged,

his thought processes, his mind-set, his living standards and his environment have undergone a sea change. Man, through a process of trial and error, has discovered the importance of Vastu Shastra for improving the living conditions in his abode for deriving peace of mind, health, tranquility and prosperity.

Vastu also guides us on how to live in harmony with our surroundings by rearranging the interiors in a house without making any structural changes.

The book contains practical tips and advice on how Vastu Shastra guides us in creating a healthy and harmonious living and working environment.

The book, *The Art of Blissful Living* gives very traditional (Paramparik), but convincing explanations to establish that Nature, Man and their combined products are governed by an evolutionary network guided by performance standards and common sense. Vedic knowledge is not a matter of research. We are attempting to carry out research, but are ignorant of our basic senses! We need to accept the fact that ultimately, perfect knowledge stems from the learnings enumerated in the following quote from the '*Bhagavad Gita*';

> **"I was born in the darkest ignorance, and my spiritual master opened my eyes with the torch of knowledge"**

During the course of my forty years of professional experience as an Architect and Vastu Advisor, I have had many opportunities in India and abroad to study and deal with people having diverse cultural and social styles of modern living. I have been privy to the problems faced by them with respect to their factory, business establishment, commercial premises, offices, workhouses, homes, etc. I have endeavoured to discuss some of these practical issues in my books.

I have also kept in view the demands made at various

International Conferences by the western people to know more about the Indian philosophy, with particular reference to Vedic Science and their application to Modern Living standards.

During the course of my studies and my professional life, I have always taken a keen interest in ancestral culture and habitat, particularly those of the most ancient Vedic Period. It has been fascinating to dig out valuable data, which proves that the living style of our ancestors was really scientific and in accordance with Vedic Principles. A lot of research work has been put in to ascertain as to how Vedic Culture could be applied to our modern living to enjoy beneficial and healthy living.

The rise of Vedic Knowledge and its subsequent applications in later periods has been taken into account. I do not wish to go into the controversy of the exact period of the Vedic Age. Indian culture and civilization are basically spiritual in nature.I quote a Sanskrit Shloka to explain about the relationship between mind and body.

Sanskrit Shloka

> "Na pranena na apranena martyo jivati Kaschana,
> Itarena tu jivanti yasmin etavapasritau".
>
> **Meaning :** Our life system is not dependent merely on the process of breathing. The intake of diet is indeed important for health, but health does not rest on food alone. The entire system can be thrown out of gear if the mind is upset. A mild turbulence injected into the mind is enough to disturb the entire balance of personality.

Your strength is in you. Religion begins where science ends; the beginning of the higher wisdom.

Accomplishment of Vedic Gyaan includes development of a relationship between the 'situation', namely our surroundings, climate, landform, view, topography, lights and its manifestations, colours etc., and the 'medium': material and construction techniques.

Design is a learning process. Man, his surroundings and the methods used are integral to each other and therefore, any design action is relative and requires the application of holistic, meditative and creative processes.

Similarly, nature, man and product are within an evolutionary network guided by performance standards. Vedic Culture is to be seen, felt, perceived, conceived and experienced from inside as well as from outside. It has to have a fourth dimension. However, it is essential to go into a very deep and careful study to understand its implications.

When we talk about Vedas, we are talking about knowledge; therefore, the mind is the main author of all our actions and behavior.

Human beings take birth on this planet based on the composition of the five elements of nature. We take birth with five senses, but it is essential to develop these five senses through knowledge. Knowledge comes from the Vedas and Development comes from the mind.

We may possess the best of knowledge; but the use of this knowledge is not through Karmas (action). It is our mind - which assimilates this knowledge and puts it to proper use.

In other words, the mind is the author, the principal, the thinker, the planner, the subject as well as the object, behind all our actions. If so, why not discuss about the mind, with the mind, for the mind. The mind that is ageless and requires no rest.

As we gain experience and advance in age, our body becomes old and weak, but our mind matures as age advances.

I, therefore, decided to pen down my experiences with the aid of Vedic Knowledge. My books are a practical guide to attain an ageless mind, with the help of the spiritual laws of Vedic Knowledge and derive the benefits through the Art of Blissful Living.

The basic reason, which has prompted me to take up the task of writing this book, is that I have been receiving numerous letters and enquiries on a daily basis from people who are seemingly confused about what is right and what is wrong while applying the Principles of Vedic Culture. The recent profusion of articles and books available on the subject of Vedic Culture in the market has added to the confusion with contradictory information, rather than providing a solution to the problem.

This state of affairs, coupled with the tremendous faith vested in me by the people around me, has motivated me to make an attempt to clarify my readers about some practical points which will help them to understand how and where to apply the Principles of Vedic Culture.

I was also keen to find answers to the question as to why there is this sudden, overwhelming interest in ancient Vedic Knowledge, not only in India, but all over the world.

This compilation is a humble attempt to discover the synchronization of Vedic Knowledge with Vastu Shastra Present-day life in the 21st Century has become complicated, illogical and contradictory.

Any attempt to describe this period fully would run into volumes, yet the end would still be nowhere in sight!

I have attempted to take a microscopic section from the magnificent Vedic period based on 'Truth' and scientific reason to show how close people are to Nature, and how they could learn the art of meaningful and fruitful living, aided by Vedic knowledge, to enjoy the gift of nature.

I am aware of the difficulties and limitations set in the path of any enterprise to seek learning from the Vedas and Upanishads. Such a venture, despite best efforts, cannot claim to be a comprehensive study of such a vast ocean of knowledge. Our aim has to be the discovery of the 'Truth', and in order to attain this goal, we must apply our minds fearlessly and without prejudice or preconception and formulate our conclusions on the basis of available evidence as far as they permit us to do so. To achieve the desired benefit in true spirit, great care is to be taken to distinguish clearly the 'Known' from the 'unknown' and to approach the 'Unmanifest' from 'Manifest'.

Vedas regulate the relation between man and his environment. A learner should exhibit his skill by overcoming the difficulties and differences between the principles laid down in the 'Vedas' and the need of the present-day requirements, keeping in mind the original relation between man and nature and to find acceptable solutions.

For good results it is all the more important to put the correct questions rather than to find the correct answers to the wrong questions.

We have to create harmony between the common values, moral codes, individual beliefs, ideological convictions, economic conditions, social obligations and cultural symbolizations coupled with philosophical ideas and meaningful environment. During the Vedic period, people built homes, temples and hermitages not merely to be used as shelter but mainly with a view to have a peaceful place for offering prayers, find peace and to live in common harmony.

The ancient philosophic concept represents two different logical processes the 'Inductive' and 'Deductive'. The former took its stand upon 'Smriti' or reasoned knowledge and law of cause and effect; and the latter dependent upon insight or inspiration, known as 'Shruti' or divine revelation of which the Vedas are said to be the expression. In modern language we may call these as an objective or atheistic and subjective or theistic science, towards the finer and subtler aspects of life and consciousness.

One ponders over answers to vital questions like: What was the beginning? How does the Universe evolve? What is the real constitution of a human being? What is the ultimate? etc.

The Vedas proclaim that the consciousness, the Universal Will, the Omnipresent and the Omnipotent 'Brahma' (Purusha) is without beginning or end.

The 'Eternal' contains Space (Akash), Time (Kala), Energy (Pran) and Nature (Prakriti). The all-pervading consciousness regulates the entire cosmos and illuminates or gives a spark of life to all individual beings. Death and decay are the source of new creation.

The Vedas propound that apart from the physical body; an individual constitutes his mind and his intellect and is presided over or enlivened by the Cosmic Consciousness. The mind function is two fold, to acquire knowledge through the five senses (Gyan Indrias) and to act in the world outside through the five related organs (Karam Indrias). The five basic elements of nature, namely, the 1.Space, 2.Air, 3.Fire, 4.Water and 5.Earth correspond to the sensations of 1.Hearing, 2.Smell, 3.Sight, 4.Taste and 5.Touch, respectively. Intellect is the discriminating power in us, to take a decision for elevation to righteousness or to indulge in sensual short-lived pleasures; to endeavor to rediscover alpha and omega of the Reality or to succumb to desires and remain in worldly illusions.

Our existence comprises of three stages of awareness: waking, dream and deep sleep stages. We also have three behavioral qualities: 'Satvic', 'Rajas' and 'Tamas'; i.e. spiritual, psychological or merely physical ways of living. We are taught that, through knowledge, selfless service and by meditation we can achieve the ultimate. Knowledge can be derived from 'Yantras', creativity from 'Tantras', energies from 'Mantras' and inspiration from 'Meditation'; the secret laws of nature.

I have combined all these together in Vedic culture to achieve best results. Despite materialistic development, resources and riches, the Westerners are looking to the Orient for desired peace of mind.

An open secret, relatively unknown, is that India is a source, the fountainhead of the vast ancient Vedic knowledge available on the planet today. When the Vedic concept is presented through modern technological advances, the sublime information becomes available to all walks of life and can be easily understood. This would give a new outlook to the world of modern living with high thinking.

Scientific explanations and Sanskrit Shlokas with their meaning, wherever possible, have been inducted to project the genuineness of the subject.

I would also like to stress that:

If we have to equip ourselves to meet the challenges of the future, we must examine the forces that are now transforming the living activity and thoughts of the people. However, in the modern world, people built concrete clusters mainly for high rate of return.

After the second World War, the architectural practices have turned out to be a race towards the so called modernization, adopting bureaucratic values, resulting in world wide pollution, environmental and ecological problems, with no peace of mind under any kind of shelter.

Sanskrit Shloka: -

Sukham Dhanani Budhimsch Santati Servadanrinam I
Priyanesham ch Sansidhim Servasyat Shublaxanam II

Yatra Nindit laxmatra tahitesham vidhakrit I
Athservamupadeyam Yabhdavet Shubhlaxanam II

Deshah purniwashch Sabhavisam Sanani Ch I
Yadyadidrisamanyashch Tathashreyaskaram Matam II

Vastusahstradritetasya Na Syallaxannirnayah I
Tasmat Lokasya Kripya satmetbhaduriyate II

Meaning : Properly designed and pleasing house will be an abode of good health, wealth, family, peace and happiness. Negligence of the canons of Vastu Principles will result in bad name, loss of fame, sorrow and disappointments. Vastu Shastra is, therefore, brought into light in favour of, to the satisfaction of, and for the betterment and overall peace and welfare of the Universe.

Vedas are the foundation of Civilization and if the foundation is not correct, good results can never be achieved. Vastu is our heritage. Heritage is like roots to a tree. So we have to go to the roots and study the most elementary and important principles of Vedas for a healthier and prosperous life, particularly in modern living. The goal of the discourses is to successfully harness the resources of heritage and give strength to the individual and thereby to the community as a whole.

The Vastu Professional should know Vedas. He should be intellectually aware of the highest truth formulated in religion. The subject of Vastu Shastra is one among several sacred sciences derived from the highest metaphysical principles. The Vastu practitioner should put in sincere efforts to acquire this comprehensive, farsighted and timeless wisdom.

Research Institute of Vedic Culture has been established to give answers to all the questions. The students and scholars of this Institution are busy doing their Research Thesis on Vedic Culture and Occult Sciences.

In the 3rd edition of the book I would like to share with the readers the importance of orientation of a building not only for saving energy but also to have a healthy design, which not only gives comfortable living but also gives good health, prosperity to the house owners/occupiers and their families.

There lies a correlation between the rotational scenario of the planets and the house designs and the different activities in the house placed in different directions with respect to the North.

The science dealing with sunshine and the effects of its intensity per given area, its rotation around the sun, earth tilt at 23 ½ degree towards the sun, Earth's attraction by the moon coupled with its environs, as its meteorological data, sea behavior, ice caps in North and South poles, rainfall, soil data, space track of the earth etc. has to be referred and studied deeply to understand the effects on human mind, body and soul in relation with the building and its environment and surrounding.

During the Vedic period, man had discovered how to utilize and improve upon the living conditions of his habitat for perpetual prosperity with the help of Vastu Shastra as described in the 'YAJURVEDA'. The Vedic principles dealing with building designs and construction existed before the *Mahabharata* and they had been practiced by our ancient architects like *Vishvakarama*. They have such a wide variety, that could be achieved only by collaboration and integration with the most modern high technology of building sciences fused with vedic sciences. A glimpse into the Vedic Sciences has been described and dealt in depth by the same author in his earlier book titled *Vedic Architecture and Art of Living*-volume I.

The Author is writing another book titled, **"Life before Death" Vol- II**. The idea behind writing this book is to make the life of the people healthy, prosperous and peaceful till they breathe last.

Despite materialistic development, resources and riches, the westerners are looking to the Orient for desired peace of mind. India is a source, the fountainhead of the vast ancient

Vedic knowledge available on the planet today. This open secret is relatively unknown. When the Vedic concept is presented through modern technological advances, the sublime information becomes available for all walks of life and be easily understood. This would give a new outlook to the world of **Life before Death**.

This is a humble attempt in giving a glimpse of habitation and the way of life in the ancient India. As far as possible, my submissions on the inter relationship of Death vis a vis Art of Living in unison with the Nature as expounded in the Vedic age, are supported by diagrams, charts, illustrations and photographs.

The views expressed in this book are strictly personal and do not reflect anybody's opinion.

The Greatest Discovery Of Mankind Is That A Human Being Can Change, Alter Or Mould His Life By Altering His Attitude Through His Trained Mind.

Prof Dr B B Puri

(Author)

1

Vedantic Thought's

To rejuvenate my soul, I regularly visit Rishikesh and stay at Parmarth Niketan. One day while sitting on the bank of the river Ganga, observing the flow of the water and the speed at which it was flowing from North to South, it struck my mind that for thousands of years the river was religiously following the routine i.e, starting its journey from Gangotri to finally merge with the Sea, covering thousands of miles in the process. The cycle of evaporation of water from the Sea and formation of clouds over Himalayas, causing rain and snowfall takes the shape of huge glaciers. The glaciers melt drop by drop and take the shape of river Ganga that starts its journey towards the Sea to merge with it.

So, whether our life also follows the same cycle of taking birth, learning, earning, eating, enjoying and thinking about life after death, we seem to be more concerned to know about the future i.e, **life after death**. We spend a lot of time and energy to find an answer to this question. Numbers of intellectuals and spiritual leaders have tried to explain the concept through their findings and experiences but a proper answer to **The Cycle of Life and Life After Death** is yet to come.

The distinction is between the eternal spirit soul and the changing material body. As the embodied soul continually passes into material body from childhood to youth to old age, the soul similarly passes into another body at death. Because we are conditioned by material nature. (Earth, Water, Fire, Air & Sound.)

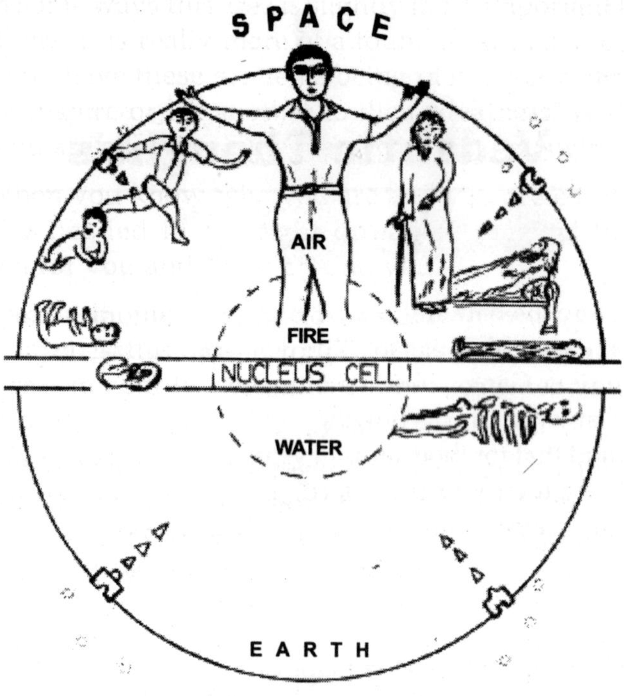

THE CYCLE OF LIFE

While sitting on the bank of Holy-river (Ganga) I was lost in my thoughts, trying to figure out as to whether there is Life After Death.

Suddenly I heard a soft but powerful voice inviting my attention. When I turned my head on to my right, I saw a saint standing very close to me. He asked me as to why I was worried about the future and trying to find an answer to the fact that there is Life After Death or not.

I was surprised, How come he came to know about my thoughts. Before I could regain my posture, he said to me, "My son, come to the present and live in the present. Do your duties properly and diligently, for what you have been sent here by the God. If you do your duties sincerely and truthfully you will build your own future accordingly. Your next birth (punarjanam) is based on your present Karmas".

The saint disappeared after saying; "It is time for my Sadhna now".

Then and there I decided to write about my experiences of Life Before Death.

2

Life
A Consciousness

Preamble

It is a misconception that 'Nature' is hostile to man. If approached in true harmony, its secrets can be revealed and the energies harnessed for the benefit of the living beings. But any relation of competition and conquest is not only unproductive but ultimately leads to environment and ecological disparities, which is 'unnatural'.

The ancient philosophical concept represents two different logical processes the inductive and deductive. The former took its stand upon 'Smriti' or reasoned knowledge and the law of cause and effect and the latter depended upon insight or inspiration, known as 'Shruti' or divine revelation, of which the Vedas are said to be the highest expression. In the modern language, we may call these as objective or atheistic science and subjective or theistic science towards the finer and more- subtler aspects of life and consciousness.

The specialist approach of the objective sciences has developed during the last three hundred years of the scientific and industrial revolution and the post World War (1945) management and information development.

The scope of research is strictly within the physical phenomena. (Incidentally, one finds these developments in the cold regions of the world where absolute physical survival is of critical priority for life to sustain and manifest. Nature is hostile to man and the man-nature relations are of competition and conquest.)

In the holistic approach, the physical and metaphysical, theistic and atheistic man, environment, objectives, mediums, tools are all considered as inseparable whole, because each is a part of, and a cause of, the evolutionary process of this great act of cosmic creative cycle. Here too, one finds clear scope and 'thresholds' of specialized fields, but, at all the scales, the central theme is holistic, and one is constantly reminded of being 'the part within the part, the whole around the whole, the universe within the universe' concept. The contexts of CONSCIOUSNESS, LIFE and MAN are complementary, constant and central. This is also called 'sub tropical science'. (One finds this culture develops around the tropical and sub tropical river valleys, where physical survival was not critical due to friendly eco-cultural relationships. Evolution of Mind and Spirit takes natural priority. The 'physical' does not pose apparent limitations for life and living. It only remains an essential base from where one takes off or the journey towards the finer and more - subtle aspects of life and consciousness.)

These are various thought processes. There was further development into Puranas. Arts, sciences and technologies also developed to highly refined levels. Mathematics, astronomy, astrology, arts, literature, music, dance, sculpture, painting, medicine, metallurgy, etc. also developed to similar levels. (Interestingly, development of long span structures did not catch attention, probably because the local weather did not need these.) Hindu, Jaina and Buddhist are three major processes of architecture and town planning in India among the Vedic creations.

EVOLUTION

One ponders to find answers to vital questions like:

What was the beginning of the beginning?
(PURUSHA) Man
How did all these evolve? (PRAKRITI) Nature
How can one distinguish relevant from irrelevant?
What is the ultimate?

There are many questions in which the 'atheists' and the 'rationalists' are equally interested. Both have theories. And, the important ones are also parallel. But many questions remain unanswered. Also, the paradox is that the more one is informed, the less he knows!

If there was 'nothing' before the beginning, how did anything begin?

Vedas say:

The Vedas proclaim that Consciousness, the Universal Will, is without Beginning or End. Paramatman. The Eternal-contains space (Akash), Energy (Prana), Mass (Rayi), Time (Kala), Movements (Gati), Transformation (Parivarthan), AtmaPurusha (Individual consciousness) and Nature (Prakriti).

The all-pervading consciousness regulates the entire cosmos and illumines or gives spark of life to all individual beings. Death and decay are the source of new creation.

There is the law of creation, the law of maintenance and evolution and the law of dissolution. Briefly, the rudiments of Vedantic thoughts can be depicted in 'Trimurti', namely, (Ref. Diag. No. 2.1:)

'Brahma', the Creator;
'Vishnu', the Sustainer; and
'Mahesh', the Annihilator

Diag. 2.1 : TRIMURTI

The Universe is governed by the positive laws. It has innumerable names and forms, that are constantly changing, moving within transformations, Ever fresh, even death and destruction are the source of new creations.

Time, movements, transformations, informations, thoughts, creation, destruction exist ever since. **LIKE DESIGN EXISTS EVER SINCE.**

The Mind is the unique creation of the Great Designer. To enjoy this grand play of consciousness, the Leela of Purusha and Prakriti, one has to observe it, discover it, create out of it and merge into it again. The "Adwaitas" call this a singular play of consciousness. The "Dwaitas" call this the Dance between the Mind and Consciousness. This is the game of Creation.

MIND is the author and the Lord of man's Inner being and the physical world around.

THE ATTITUDE

The Vedantic learning process insists on reminding constantly along the following principles:-

This is in the form of peace invocation chanted before commencement of every lesson. This deals with the holistic attitude, the need to constantly work together in a team.

These are reproduced below:-

Sanskrit Shloka

Purnamadah Purnamidam Purnatpurnam Udachyate, Purnasya Purnamadaya, Purnameva Vashishyate Om, Shanti, Shanti, Shanti!

Ref. Diag. No. 2.2

Meaning

This is perfect, that is perfect and from the perfect, the perfect emerges. If perfect, only the perfect remains. Om, Peace, Peace, Peace!

Sanskrit Shloka: -

"Sahanavavatu Sahanaubhunakty Sahaveeryam Karavavahai,
tjaswina Wadhitamastu Ma Vidvishavavahai
Om, Shanti, Shanti, Shanti !"

Meaning: -

Let Him protect us both, May be blessed with the bliss of knowledge, Let us do the brave act together, May our studies be thorough and faithful. May we not ever misunderstand each other. Oh: Eternity: Peace: Peace: Peace.

त्रिगुणात्मक माया

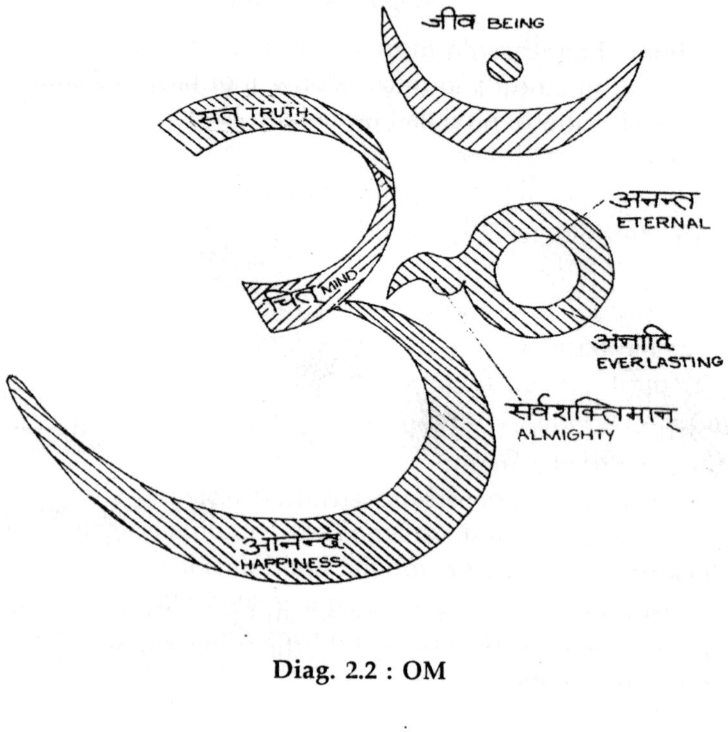

Diag. 2.2 : OM

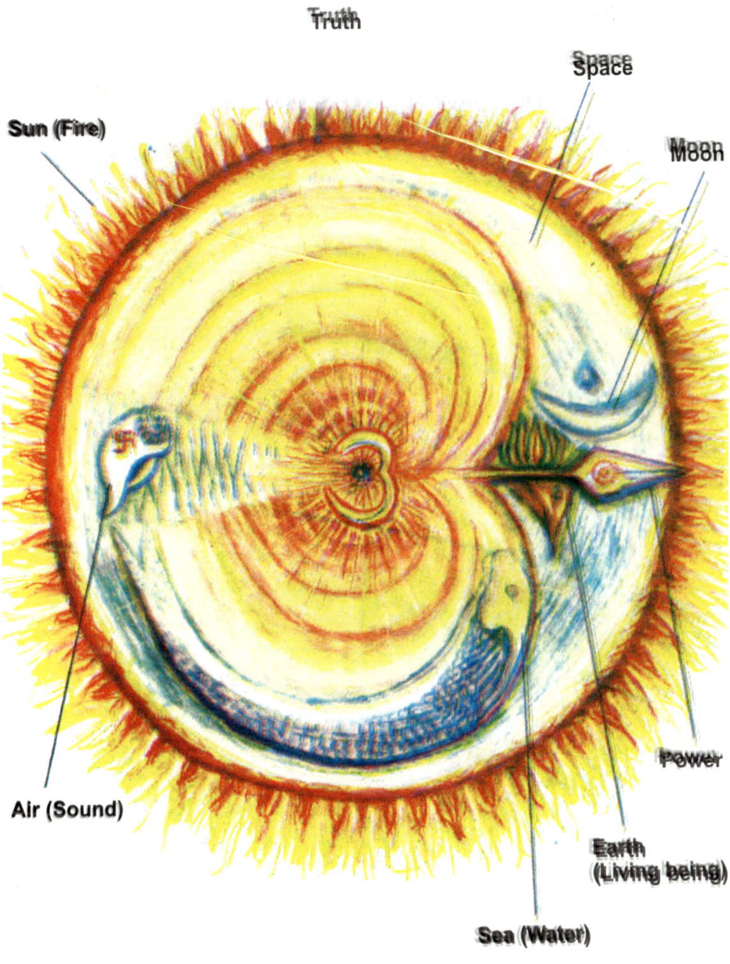

Diag. 2.3

Originally painted by Prof B B Puri

The last two lines are a warning towards the possible lack of accuracy and thoroughness of 'the Generalist'. Also, that the lack of communication may result in misunderstanding or misapplication of information or knowledge to design. Thorough understanding, right application and meaningful communication are important to team work. (Holistic is not generalist. In order to keep the total balance, it has to be very accurate.)

OM

'OM' a Healing Mantra represents the eternal endlessness of universe (time and space) and so, endlessness of knowledge and information. The utterance of 'Shanti' three times after 'OM' is essential for peace and tranquility (necessary for learning) from three sources of disturbances, from within, from surroundings and from disturbances beyond human control. (Ref. Diag No. 2.2)

The concept of 'OM', the Mahamantra as visualised by the author while on regular meditation and uttered (Japa) in the 'SAMADHI' posture (Sthiti), produces such an enormous and powerful vibration that it virtually gives emergence to the five elements, viz., Space, Air, Fire, Water and Earth, of which the entire Shrishti is composed. This imagination of the author is unique and has been thoroughly and comprehensively bought out in Diag. No. 2.3.

Starting from the vacuum or the void "SHUNYA" with the utterance of 'OM', its vibration spreads enormously to infinity.

The sound wave that emanates from the void has been represented by 'SHANKH' and also represents Air. It goes on magnifying and constitutes space, water, earth and ultimately produces fire, which give the meditator, power ('SHAKTI') and when all these combine together they generate into 'SHRISHTI' and this originates 'Life and Vegetation' in the universe.(Diag No. 2.4)

Diag. 2.4

'Air'	or sound wave is represented by 'SHANKH'
'Water'	or sea is represented by Fish 'Meen'
'Space'	the vibrations make the infinity
Samadhi	To sit with folded legs on the ground in one posture for 'Japa'. (Sthiti)
Shankh	Sea Shell through which sound is produced and is mostly used before or after Yajna, Puja of Prayer. The sound produced by Shankh is said to purify the atmosphere to the extent the sound reaches.

Shriśhti	Creation of the entire Universe
'Earth'	represented by 'Life and Vegetation'
'Fire'	represented by the hot and ever- glowing 'Sun which gives heat, light and energy to all.

THE MANTRA, THE YANTRA AND THE TANTRA

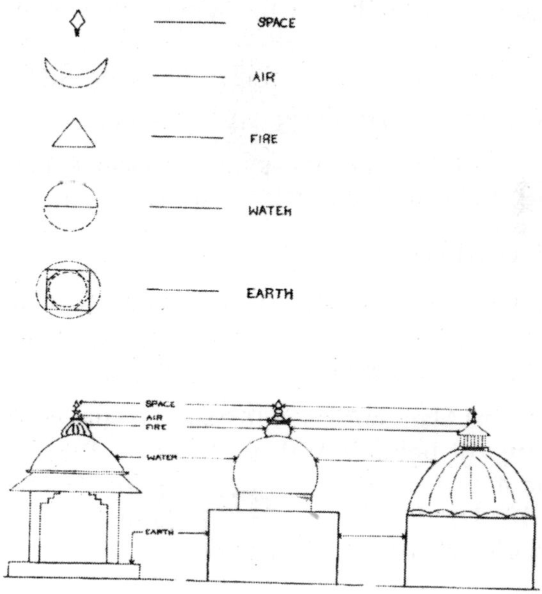

Diag. 2.5

To any activity, there are three aspects: 'Mantra' or Concept, 'Yantra' or the instruments, tools, or mediums, and 'Tantra': the administration of the act of creation.

In the beginning of creation, the Supreme Personality of Godhead expands Himself in the form of Purusha incarnation of Maha- Vishnu. Lying in the Causal Ocean, Maha-Vishnu impregnates the living entities into material nature by glancing over His unmanifest material energy (shown here as the Goddess Durga). The word 'Durga' signifies "prison" and it is Goddess Durga's function to see that all sinful souls are kept within the prison of this material world.

For this purpose, Lord Krishna has given Durga so much power that she can create, maintain and annihilate the cosmos. Diag. No. 2.5

IMAGINATION, TOOLS AND SKILLS

Through understanding of 'the Systems' and 'the Methods', an object attains its gross or subtle form or meaning, depending upon the 'LEVEL OF LIFE EVOLUTION' of the 'KNOWER'.

These levels or 'SHEATHS' are five-fold: -

Gross Matter / Vital Air Energy / Mental- Emotional / Intellectual / Judiciary / Bliss / spiritual / Total communication.

THE TOTAL MAN

According to the Upanishads, an average human has five senses and a super human intellectual man can open his sixth sense, called 'The Third Eye of Cosmic Vision'.

The Perfect Man consists of 16 Kalas, 3 states of awareness and 3 states of behavioural qualities. 1. Prana 2. Faith 3. Akasha 4. Air 5. Fire 6. Water 7. Earth 8. The Senses 9. Mind 10. Food 11. Strength 12. Thought 13. Mantra 14. Karma 15. The World 16. Names.

Three Awareness States are: -

1. Awake
2. Dream and
3. Sleep

Three behavioural states are: - Tamas, Rajas and Satva.

Man, above all, is a tool making instrument. He communicates and expands beyond his physical frame through mind, spirit, smell and instrumentations. This quality of man needs to be guided for positive co-existence. His various faculties can be trained and disciplined for the highest efficiency, positive co-existence and creative efforts.

Now, let us understand the Nature-Man-and surrounding transfer process. If man is the reflection of Nature, the nature reflects man and his total personality (PURUSHA). Human body and mind complex are instruments, which communicate, absorb, expand and get consumed in the nature. Nature, Man and surroundings are the natural evolutionary extensions of one another, forming a complete whole.

The process of Transfer is briefly explained in Diag. No. 2.6.

BASIC FIVE SENSES OF MAN AND CORRESPONDING CO-RELATION WITH COSMOS

Five Senses	**Hearing**	**Touch**	**Sight**	**Taste**	**Smell**
The Basic Elements	Space	Air	Fire	Water	Earth
Instruments of Perception (To acquire inward)	Ears	Skin	Eyes	Tongue	Nose
Work Organs (To act outward)	Speech Commu. (Exit)	Hands Work (Finger)	Feet Mobility	Anus Discard	Genitals Procreate
Control Centres	Mind (Flow of thoughts or Emotion)	Intellect (Power of Discrimination)			
The Presiding Force	The Cosmos Consciousness or Supreme Energy, 'Prana' or the life force.				
Transforms Landscape	(a) Silence	Climate	Light	Plumbing	
related Technological	(b) Accoustics	Weather Conditioning	Colour	Cooling	Flora
	(c) Vibrations		Texture	Texture Surfaces	Repose/ forms
Odour					
	(d) The Concept or spirit of the project.				
Universal Graphic Symbols					

Diag. 2.6

3

Foundation of Indian Civilization

Philosophy of Life

The aim of the Vedic philosophy was to discover first, the secret laws of the Universe and then from them to shape a pattern of every-day life. The Indo-Aryan village was, therefore, conceived of as a universe in itself, on a small scale. The five social grades partly based upon race and partly upon occupation, were the four recognized Varnas, known as the 'pure classes' the Brahmins, the Kshatriyas, the Vaishyas and the Shudras and the fifth class comprising the offspring of inter-marriages not recognized by the Aryan law.

These 'five peoples' of the Aryan community represented the five elements of the universe, and each had a part of the village assigned to it, symbolizing a small division of that universe.

The Brahmins (Priests) acquired the most prominent place among the five peoples or 'Panch-Jana'. At birth, the Brahmin stood on a level common to the Kshatriya, Vaishya and Shudra.

It was only at the ceremony of investiture with the sacred thread and initiation into the state of Brahmacharya or studentship, when his spiritual father, the Brahmin guru, whispered in his ear the mystic formula, the Gayatri Mantra, which contained the essence of all the Vedas, that he was born to Brahmin-Hood.

The Kshatriyas formed the Aryan fighting clans. Their specific duty was the protection of the whole community and the administration of justice. Though they were the ruling community, they were ranked lower than the Brahmins - the spiritual leaders of the people.

The Vaishya class, which included agriculturists, traders and craftsmen, was not bound by such strict rules of morality as the two upper classes, since money lending were 'Satyanrita' or mixture of truth and falsehood. Yet, the ancient code of Aryan ethics declares that "of all pure things, purity within acquiring wealth is pronounced as the most excellent. Since he who gains wealth with clean hands is truly pure. Even in Vedic times, the trading community was an influential one among the Aryans in India.

Shudras were the lowest of the four classes not recognized as 'Pure' as Aryans. They were not permitted to wear the sacred thread, the symbol of a second or spiritual birth, and their highest duty, according to 'Manu' was the service of the Brahmins, with the expectation that if faithfully performed, it might bestow on for them Brahmin-hood in the next birth.

Outside the four Varnas, but still included within the Aryan pale was a fifth class called Samanya or common alias Sutas, which was formed by irregular inter-marriages between the other classes or between the Aryans and the Non - Aryans.

Every member of the Brahmin, Kshatriya and Vaishya family, wearing the sacred thread or 'Yajnopavita' was supposed to perform religious duties. "The morning Sandhya includes various practices bathing in the running water, breathing exercises, and recitation of the Gayatri Mantra, the most sacred of all formulae (Mantras)."

SANSKRIT Shloka : " Om bhur bhuvah svah
Tat Savitur Varenyam
Bhargo Devasya dhimahi
Dhiyo Yo nah prachodayat".

Meaning:- The first line contains Om, the mighty monosyllable, the Alpha and Omega of all reality, followed by the names of the three octosyllabic lines from the Rigveda: "That desirable glory of the God Savitur, may we possess it. It will awaken our thoughts", and other Vedic texts. Then five "great sacrifices" (Mahayajna) - offering to the Gods (deva), demons (bhuta), and ghosts of the dead (pitri), to men (nri) by the exercise of hospitality, and to the Brahmin by the reading of Vedic texts.'

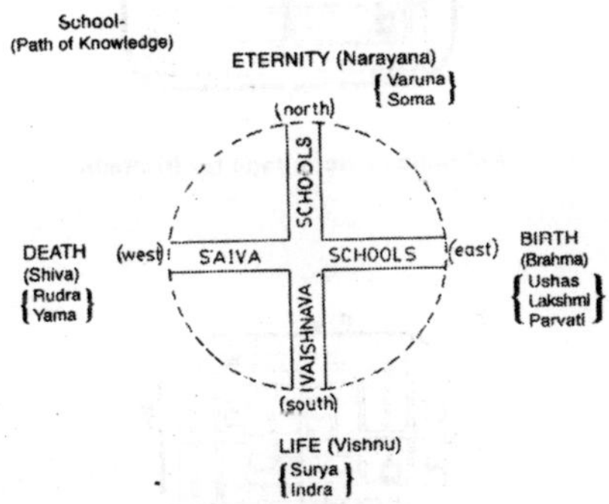

Brahma, Vishnu and Shiva (Mahesh) may be regarded as collective names standing for all the symbols, which are associated with Birth, Life and Death in the abstract. Nirvana may be taken as a collective name for all the symbols of Future life and eternity. The orientation symbolized by sunrise, sunset, noon and midnight.

Diag. 3.1 : THE SYMBOL OF COSMIC CROSS

After that honour is paid to the five idols of the home (ayatana) symbolizing Vishnu, Siva, Durga, Ganesha, and Surya morning and in evening there is an agnihotra, a sacrifice of fire.

The sandhya, or daily ritual of the Brahmin, performed at sunrise, noon, and sunset, also belongs to the immemorial traditions of the Aryan way of life, in which the sun was worshipped as the symbol of the unknown power in the universe, governing all other natural powers. This tradition grew up with the organization of the Aryan village, in which Mangalavith, i.e. a path surrounding the village, was consecrated for the performance of the rite of Pradakshina , symbolizing the path of the sun across the heavens or the turning of the wheel of life and death. (COSMIC CROSS - refer to Diag. No. 3.1)

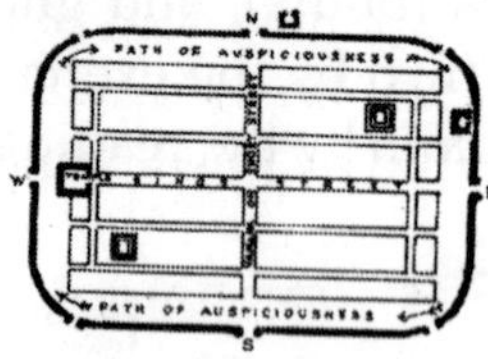

Ashrama or Hermitage for Brahmin

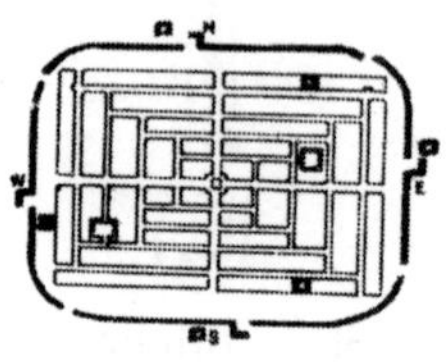

For a mixed population including all the tour Varnas. (corrected for Ram Raj Architecture of Hindus)

Diag. 3.2 : INDO-ARYAN VILLAGE PLAN

The sites of the villages were carefully chosen according to principles. First, ritualistic - governed by the Indo - Aryan rites as discussed earlier, and, second, sanitary, as expounded in the Shilpa Shastras and observed in the traditions of the Indo - Aryan master builder. The villages were generally situated on the riverbanks, by the seashore or by the side of a lake, not only because of the requirement of the agrarian

Aryan Community but because of the ample bathing facilities provided by them. Bathing was regarded as a religious rite in itself, and a necessary preliminary for sacrificial rites. A stream was always preferred to the stagnant one out of sanitary considerations. The 'Devas' or the 'Shining ones', who were the guardian spirits of the Aryan people, loved the places, which by Nature or by careful planning, were provided with water and pleasant gardens, on the North East side of the Village as per the Vastu Shastra.

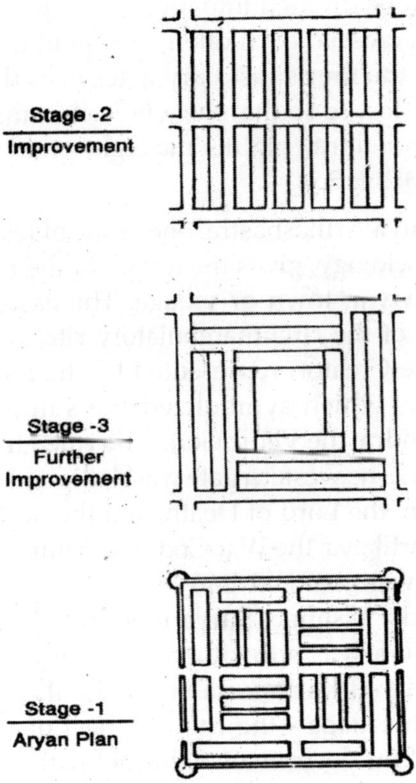

Evolution of Vedic Plan for Contemporary Architecture

Diag. 3.3 : ARYAN VILLAGE PLANNING (much early period)

The Aryan way of life gave rise to the symbolism, which also became an inseparable aspect of the Indo-Aryan villages. We find the philosophy of an individual mingled with his total environment. Such a unique inter-relation of a man and his town is not to be found anywhere in the world. The expounders of the Shilpa Shastras have done a commendable job in moulding the religious philosophy in the physical forms of the village planning. The typical form, probably derived from the fortified camp of the early Aryans, was a rectangular enclosure with its four sides facing the four quarters, divided into four wards by the two main streets, which crossed each other sectors in the centre and terminated at the four subsidiary gates near the corners of the village enclosure so that the whole circumstance of the walls was divided into eight - 'the eight - fold path'. (Refer to Diag. No. 3.2 & 3.3)

The Kautilya Arthashastra, one of the oldest treatises on politics and sociology, gives the names of the four principal gates of the Aryan town or village. The eastern gate, the starting point of the circumambulatory rite, was dedicated to Brahma, the Creator, represented by the rising sun. The southern gate, which symbolized the sun at noon, was dedicated to Indra, the Vedic God, who ruled the firmament during the day. The western gate was dedicated to the setting sun, or to Yam, the Lord of Death, and the northern gate to Senapati or Kartikeya, the War God. The nature of symbolism of the Vedas was changed into the philosophic concept of the Upanishads. Vishnu - Surya took the place of Indra at the Zenith, Siva was substituted for Yam and Vishnu - Narayana replaced Karthikeya. It was on this symbolic rite of Indo-Aryan village - the rite of wheel of life - that the Buddha based his doctrine of eight-fold path.

The Vedic way of life was, thus, the moving spirit of the organization of the Aryan Village communities. The Indian lore is full of laws given in crystallized form by saints and scholars in every branch of learning.

The process by which such universal laws were arrived at may be unknown to us, but these formulae, in most cases, are found perfect and are applicable even today. Nothing was left undirected. The execution of even the minutest detail had laws governing it.

The principles laid down for the construction of dwellings, even today, seem amazingly scientific. The religious mystery given to the whole process gave birth to superstitions that generally arise from exaggerating a logical reasoning. The religious connotation was probably employed to keep the law makers (kings) and the Brahmins (priests) from being transparent. Rituals gave the whole process a sacred dimension, which saw to it that every little detail was efficiently carried out.

Dwelling on The Principles of Vastu Shastra

While creating a dwelling, the basic idea was always to recreate symbolically an Universe. It was intended to adequately circumscribe a consecrated piece of ground on which to maintain during the sojourn on earth, a living contact with the transcendental principle. The concept of a house however has been changing over the times.

In the Rig Vedic period, a house was looked upon as a temple. Later (1500 BC), it was compared to a womb (as a child grows secure in a mother's womb) man prayed for the similar security and peace.

4

The Art of Living Before Death

Physical Birth to Spiritual Re-Birth

Cosmic Vision

The Hindu philosophy, the Vedas say that a human is just an animal in human form. In humans and animals, there are many common habits like eating, drinking, sleeping, sex and fear. Animals too live in groups or lairs, breed, feed and protect their offspring. Humans, in addition to similar animal instincts, build industries to live luxurious and artificial life and amass wealth. Animals live with the Nature created by God. But does all this lead to Godliness or Spiritual uplift?

It is only when a person attains spiritual awakening that he attains humanhood. Man must, therefore, awake himself.

The Hindus perform thread (Janeo) yajno-pavita ceremony and Parsis perform Navjot (new birth, or second birth). This custom goes back to the Vedic period. The ceremony then signified the initiation of the child in its eighth year to spiritual awakening.

Man must, therefore, awaken himself by mere touch of the Guru (Godman) or a Spiritual guide who can release laser rays which pierce the membrane in the middle of the eyebrow, thus opening the KUNDALINI'S, positive force, the Inward Eye as the third eye of cosmic vision.

The mother gives birth to a child, The father gives sanskar (a tradition in the society and guru (teacher) gives knowledge (gyan). I was born in the darkest ignorance, and my spiritual masters opened my eyes with the touch of knowledge.

Kundalini (Shakti or Power)

Before I explain the third Eye of cosmic vision, first of all, we have to understand what is Kundalini(a pipeline of energy like positive and negative electric wire where both voltage and currents pass). In our gross physical body, the automatic process is of breathing IN (positive) and breathing OUT (negative). The positive and negative currents pass through the Kundalini, the negative current entering the sex organs of both the male and the female from the spinal base. In females, it comes out through the ovaries releasing an ovum into the uterus.

Pregnancy occurs if and when it mates with male sperm. Otherwise, it is cast out and its energy lost. In the male, the negative current (energy) is released through the testicles, the sperms passing out through the penis.

Thus, the negative energy of Kundalini is channelised in both the male and the female through their sex organs, which God or Nature use only for procreation. When humans use sex for sensuous recreation, they divert the energy force from going upwards towards the positive opening of the Kundalini in humans alone, who have this subtle force in the spine connected to the brain with an opening, the third eye, in the front lobe. But this opening is like an eye cataract which blocks light from entering the vision unless removed. Similarly, in the case of human beings, this opening shuts out the spiritual light unless we make a positive effort to rouse the Kundalini upwards.

The unseen mysterious, Kundalini rousing process, if

simply put, is one of reversing the outgoing flow of life energy through the sex nerves by way of sperm to flow back and upwards through the spine into the brain by means of meditation which requires total control over sex consciousness.

Thus, the sperm ejected during the physical sex union is sublimated into super human power through the reversal of the process, which brings about the final spiritual orgasm, i.e., union between man and God.

The illustration shows the stage of Kudalini Shakti rising upwards from the base of the spine in the coccyx (diag. 4.1) to the third or cosmic eye at brow between the eyebrows. The symbols represent the various chakhras that open one after another around the spine to the upward thrust of Kundalini Shakti.

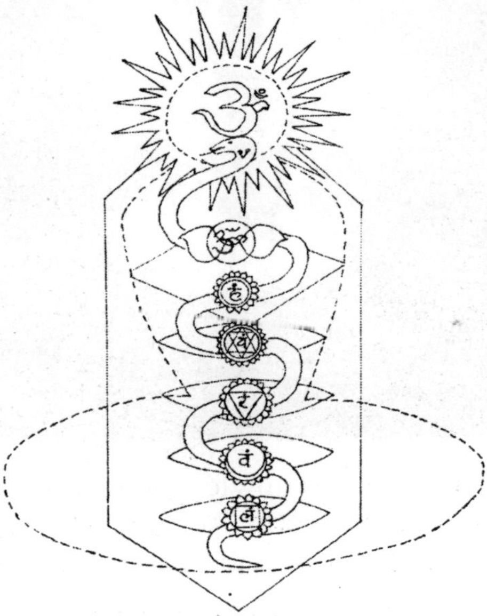

Diag. 4.1 : COCCYX

Coccyx : The last bone of the vertebral column. It is triangular in shape and curved slightly forward. It is made up of four small bones.

LORD (the Vedic knowledge) resides in His own abode, in the spiritual world. Actually, He is everywhere. He is even within the atom as the 'Paramatma' or Supersoul.

The Vedic concept describes the creation in two basic phenomena: Purusha and Prakriti.

PURUSHA is consciousness, the life source. It is also called Atman. The Paramatma or Vaishwanara (the universal consciousness), the Atman (Individual consciousness), Prana (life) and Jiva (also life or soul). Paramatman and atman are one, but represent two scales. Atman reflects as Prana or Jiva in the body through Mind. (According to Shiva Sankalpa Sutra, Mind in its purest satvika form is itself Atman.) Purusha is timeless, ageless, constant, absolute consciousness. A singular truth Adwaita. Prana is the central source of all energies in all living things, and not energy itself. Prakriti is the world of names and forms. Ever changing, evolving and operating in Dwaita. (The Duals). The dualism of positive negative, creation-destruction, good- bad, Male-Female etc.

PRAKRITI has countless forms. The Prakriti also has permanence, but of a different nature. It is in the cyclic relay order, i.e., while the species survive over the time, the body of the specie is created and destroyed and recreated again and again. So, at a given body level, it is temporary. After Prakriti comes Purusha, the life source. Purusha manifests itself in Prakriti through Ego and Ambition (Tamas and Rahas). Purusha Suktam of the Puranas describes this vivid play of Prakriti and Purusha in great detail. Thus, the Purusha is the life, the essence, the idea, the will behind any name or form the physical world, in the absence of which the physical mass, forms or systems simply crumble and decompose. Purusha is the power behind all physical existence.

The Mind

Mind is the Lord and author of man's physical world around him.

The mind mainly operates at two levels. The external (convex) mind receives and reflects all information from the Prakriti, (The external world of names and forms).The physical world consists of five elements; Space, Air, Water, Fire and Earth. These represent Sound, Touch, Taste, Sight and Smell. The sense organs are the physical instruments through which Mind communicates with the physical world. Ordinarily, mind depends on the sense organs for communication with the physical world. Thus, the mind may be fed information as per the 'interests' or conditioning of the sense organs. The objectives of sense organs are Artha, Kama and Dharma (Wealth, Comfort and Glory). The external surface of mind is in constant touch with the external world and its nature is to be mobile constantly, so as to efficiently perform its basic job to keep in touch with Prakriti information and to transmit it, i.e., to communicate.

This wandering mind is constantly wants desires and feelings of incompleteness. Always wanting but never satisfied. This makes man feel insecure, weak having lack of confidence, etc. So, man, looks for psychological and moral support all the time, viz., support of any **MEDIUM** as props, (Religion, work, people, drugs, etc.)

The Core Mind or the inner mind has the function of communicating with Purusha. However, unlike the external Mind, it does not depend on external physical sense instruments. This mind has to train itself to be self-operative. An untrained mind may feel this capacity at times, but cannot operate at will on this facility. Unlike Prakriti, Purusha is stable, timeless, ageless, continuous, pure consciousness, source of creativity, the beginning of all beginnings and life behind all Prakriti.

The inner mind is introvert, quiet and meditative, a constant source of truth, solitude and happiness. The inner mind is made of 'Satvika' aspects of the five elements and sheaths (physical, emotional, intellectual, vital energy and bliss). Its goal is to seek communication with Atman and Paramatman and merge with it when detached from the Mind body complex.

This mind never dies and has continued with time and space. The information collected, stored and processed by individual minds gets transmitted to the universal mind. One finds universal waves behaviour of people over a large geographical region.

HUMAN PROBLEMS

The human problems are of three kinds:

1) Two basic human desires: - to procure the desired and to protect the procured. This is the constant source of the feeling of insecurity. (Ambition Rajas)
2) If he can manage, he would wish to have it with no effort or minimum effort (Tamas).
3) The restless external mind is, time and again, reminded by the inner mind to hold, think. meditate, come back to the self, co-operate with the Purusha in the law of Prakriti. There is a constant struggle within the mind.

PATANJALI'S YOGA SUTRA

As solutions to the above problems, various answers or the view points have evolved, called Darshanas. The Yoga sutra avoids external mediums as far as possible (though does not bar them) and has developed Yoga technology and attitudes with the Mind- Body complex itself as medium and auto-suggestive methods. The schools are of little relevance for the purpose of evolving patterns for architectural expressions. However, it is mentioned for its importance in training of the designer's creative mental attitudes.

THE ICONS, YANTRAS AND MANDALAS

These are for visual responses of codes. These are visual symbols as mediums or invocation, Icons or Murti or statues in human forms, semi-human, animal or demonic forms. These are most popular among the visual symbols for the common people. The iconic symbols range from a human figure representing the entire universe (Vaishvanara, Viratswarupa, etc.) to various other specific energy systems to be invoked for a particular objective, such as Shakti, Lakshmi, Saraswati, Brahma, Vishnu, Shiva, etc. Each one with specific symbols is associated to represent the energies assimilated within the specific network.

KNOWLEDGE TO DESIGN OR CONCEPT

Thorough understanding, right application and meaningful communication are important teamwork. In order to keep the total balance, it has to be very accurate. For any activity, following are the three aspects: -

1. Mantra or concept
2. Yantra or mediums (instruments or tools)
3. Tantra or act of creation (administration)

THE MANTRA

Mantras are graphic symbols representing the respective energy networks. Each Yantra has its mantra as well as icon. Shri mantra, Gayatri mantra, Surya, Yogini, Vishnu, etc. All Yantras evolve patterns from a central point. This centre is considered the source of creation and the object for concentration. The concentric patterns around the centre are specific to the energy pattern one wishes to invoke. This pattern is a visual code to constantly remind the Sadhaka of the network he is meditating on.

These are for audial responses or codes. It may be monosyllable like Om, Rim, Klim, Krim, etc. or in hymn form with the combination of sounds, words, dictions of specific composition to invoke a given set of energies.

YANTRA OR MEDIUMS

Yantras are for the intellectually superior or evolved persons who may not need icons. Yantras are generally two dimensional, symmetric, concentric patterns using elementary geometric forms such as circle, square and other regular geometric polygons.

Lotus flowers varying from four to one hundred are also incorporated. Yantras can be designed and developed to represent any specific energy network. Yantras have colour codes, too.

TANTRA (KARMAKANDA AND TANTRISM)

The problem is of the relationship between the sense organs and the external mind. The mind and the senses both should be disciplined and be in harmony and awareness with Prana. Mediums and methods are developed, responding to senses and the sensuality of the Mind. First, the mind should have positive reasons and clear objectives to concentrate upon. To reach that state of stability, some intermediary mediums vehicles or catalysts are developed. These carriers are sound, touch, vision, taste and smell, since these are the factors of sense organs. The mediums or vehicles should correlate with the specific objectives. It should have the potency to reach the goal and its directions and action network to be with clear and accurate commands.

Mantras, Yantras and Tantras are developed with these considerations. In Sanskrit these are defined as:

- Protection through Mind is Mantra Sound (Concept)
- Protection through Effort is Yantra (Work)
- Protection through Crossing (Hurdles) is Tantra (Management & Methods)

Mantra is for mental conceptual efficiency. Sound (Audial Form) is its vehicle.

Yantra is for work efficiency. Vision (visual form) is its vehicle.

Tantra is for management efficiency. Process is its vehicle.

Similarly, there are specific touches; taste and smells associated with specific Mantra, Yantra and Tantra.

The above three are MEDIUM and METHODS, bridging human WILL to objectives, designed and developed for various kinds of human desires Material, Emotional, Intellectual, Vital, Bliss Tamasika, Rajasika or Sativka.

While these mediums are used to help a Sadhaka to attain initial meditation practice, these are more popular among the common people as methods to attain material goals of life. For the second group of goals, one is interested in satisfying certain specific desires such as procure and protect, wealth, comforts, glory, sensual or mental gratifications, etc. For each of these, the MEDIUMS are utilized to invoke specific set of energies in a desired pattern of network and potency. This is the real Life before Death.

5

Life Before Death or Life After Death ?

The Mystery of " The UNKNOWN" :

The Unknown is the essence of all activities of the human mind. The horizon is always a concept, because it vanishes the moment you reach that point. The Horizon has its reality in '**IMAGINATION**' or '**CREATIVITY**'. It emerges from the beginning of all the beginnings.

Every time one goes deep into the **SOURCE** and looks for the **IMPULSE**, or **RATIONALE**, a process, a method follows. Life sprouts in impulses.

Is there anything called "death" when we approach the issue seriously? What place does 'death' have in the awareness of a true Knower? What should be the right attitude of the truly awakened one in regard to life and death? These are very important questions, for; the seekers often think that the fall of the body will alone mark the consummation of spiritual evolution and attainment. There is also the view that even for the spiritual seer, continued life in the body is more botheration than otherwise.

The true vision will be neither to long for death, thinking

that death alone will be a full solution to the problems of embodiment, nor to foster any undue concern or botheration about the continuance of life. The knower should look at both life and death with this habitual equalness and indifference. What are life and death, except a pair of opposites? Like day and night, happiness and misery, success and defeat etc. these two are one set, perhaps more important, more grave and more deluding.

Life is but an event that can only follow birth. Birth relates to the body. The body gets born not because of any one of us, but because of the supreme laws of Nature governing animate existence and reproduction. The born body continues to live due to the merit of the same Natural sequence. After a time it dies, governed again by Nature's own laws. As such, on interference is called for from the truly wise man.

What is there to be so much afraid of death? Is there death at all? Equally so, what is in life to be so much longed for? Is not death a phase every one already enjoys every day? Whenever you recede from your wakeful state at the end of the day and get immersed within your body to remain lost, you are in fact put to death for a few hours. It is only that you survive the plight when you wake up and regain the normal wakefulness. The only difference between death and this 'dead spell' is that the latter is a short-living event, while the former is not.

However, the so-called death is quite within the reach of every one, in the same way as is life. In spite of the repeated deaths and continued lives, does not every one endure and preserve himself intact? Does not the 'I' in him exist and survive ever and ever? Thus, the Self in us is clearly transcendental. It is beyond both life and death.

What can then stand in your way of becoming what the 'I' in you already is? Be what you already are. As is the Truth, so too do you, the truth-knower, become and behave.

This is the last undeniable call of true spiritual wisdom. It can never be difficult for anyone to heed it in full.

Put the concept of death to further reason and see whether it can hold its own. Death becomes relevant only with its opposite, namely birth. Both of them can become relevant only when the body's existence to which they relate, proves itself as real and stands approved. Here comes all the difficulty and opposition from our own intelligence, which always looks for pure and unassailable wisdom.

If we have to think of a genuine relation between the body and the soul, it will be to think of a positive relationship between two things, which are opposed to each other. But can that be possible? Can one be alive as well as dead at the same time? Can light be present together with darkness? For us to speak of any understandable relation, basically there must be the presence of more than one thing. And the things concerned must exist together, at the same time.

How can two things, which are opposed to each other as light and darkness, be ever considered to exist together? As long as this is not possible, the idea of a relation being born and persisting between the soul and the body is absurd and untenable.

If one ever thinks of death, clearly he is still imperfect in his vision. He has not yet become fully aware of the Single Soul and its absolute nature. Truly, the question of death or destruction does not arise at all in the context of the Soul.

The presence of the soul is everywhere and in everything. Hence it is in the dead body as well, as in the living body. The right understanding of the Soul is that it is supreme, single, absolute and all pervading. That means it exists not merely in the sentient being and creatures, but also in the non-sentient, inert entities. The dead body is one such inert entity. If the whole of the universe, including the countless gross planets are nothing but the soul, is not the dead body as well as the same soul?

Nevertheless, the truth is that the Soul is present everywhere.

However, I want to stress that when the truth that the 'Soul is present even in the dead body' is accepted, where does the question of its having gone or escaped from the body and therefore having to accept another body, or say to reincarnate, arise at all? The thought of reincarnation is truly absurd and irreconcilable when you really comprehend the Soul and its absoluteness.

In fact, it is a living human who can take up reasoning and pursue it. Whether he wants it or not, his being is more sentimental and emotional than rational. Life for any one begins with sentiments and to a very large extent it also remains so till the fall of the body.

When man begins to reason, his deepest sentiments inevitably forge behind his reason on the basis of his strong sense of acceptance or rejection, preference or prejudice.

The natural outcome is that throughout the reasoning which his intelligence evolves thereafter, he will be covertly influenced by his own deep sentimental bent. The whole of his reasoning will not then take him so much to the truth as it is as to the truth as he wishes it to be.

We generally speak of the mind only in respect of living beings, particularly ourselves. Only those who are able to feel, sense and react to external provocations are considered to possess a mind. In this sense we can describe the mind as the middle entity, which reveals both inertness and sentience alike. Remaining in our body it tells us about the body's existence and its inert nature. Equally, it also reveals to us the existence of the sentient spirit or the self. Even in respect of the outside objects, it reveals to us the distinction between the inert entities and the sentient ones.

Suppose you try to search for and examine the mind in yourself, what will be the result? First of all, you will identify it as thoughts, emotions, feelings etc. if you examine the thoughts and emotions, you will reach at their units and components, which when further analysed, will take you to the deeper and finer levels. At last you will reach the deepest and finest, wherein neither will you be the examiner, nor the other, the examined, remain.

The whole process will vaporize or dissolve itself completely landing you inwardly in a unique state, which on comparison with what all you now know and feel, has to be described as nothing but the superb expression of wholeness. This wholeness comprehends among other things, your mind, intelligence, body and the objects outside, say anything and all which this visible universe enfolds within it.

The function of the Core Mind or the inner mind is to communicate with Purusha. However, unlike the Outer Mind, it does not depend on external or physical sensory instruments. This mind trains itself to be self-operative. An untrained mind may realize the presence of this capacity at times; but it does not have the capacity to operate this facility at will.

Unlike Prakriti, Purusha is stable, timeless, ageless, continuous, pure consciousness, a source of creativity, the beginning of all beginnings, the life behind all Prakriti.

The inner mind is introverted, quiet and lapse having a constant source of truth, solitude and happiness. It is made of Satvika aspects of the five elements and sheaths (physical, emotional, intellectual, vital energy and bliss). Its goal is to establish communication between Atma and Paramatma and merge it with Brahma, when detached from the mind and body complex. This mind never dies and has continuity with time and space. The information collected, stored and processed by individual minds gets transmitted to the universal over a large geographical region.

The mind collects information mainly from the two sensory organs i.e. Eyes and Ears. (What you see and what you hear).

The eyes can perform their function of seeing only when there is light within the eyes as well as outside in the environment. Only then can one see, visualize and marvel at the beauty of nature.

In darkness, when there is no light within or outside, what the eyes experience is only a sense of dark black colour.

The images seen by the eyes are stored in the mind, which in turn, processes the images and segregates them into good images and bad or unpleasant images. One likes to see the good images again and again; but would not like to see the bad images of second time.

Similarly, the ears pick up all the sound vibrations around us, be it soothing, pleasant sound or unpleasant, jarring sound. They may emanate from persons close to our hearts or from enemies. These sound vibrations are transmitted to the mind, which in turn analyses and edits the sound waves. Obviously, one would like to listen to the soothing and pleasant sounds and block the unpleasant or jarring sounds.

It is obvious from the above that the mind controls the organs of our body.

For example, you are physically present in a classroom and attentively listening to the teacher's lecture word by word. Suddenly, your mind loses its concentration and your thoughts go to a Beach Party that you had attended last month. You recall with pleasure, the fun you had with all your friends, the music, dancing, the delicious food and the spectacular view as the sun set over the ocean. You experience a lot of joy as you relive those great moments.

Suddenly, your teacher jolts you out of your reverie and pulls you up for daydreaming. You say that your attention was very much in the class. The teacher then asks you to repeat what was being said in the class. Your mind is blank, as you were not paying any attention to the lecture. You were physically present in the class, but you were neither seeing the teacher nor listening to the lecture. However, your mind was miles away at the party!

The mind plays a very important role in your past, present and future. It works tirelessly night and day, nonstop 24 hours a day. Even while your body is resting or is fast asleep, the mind is continuously working; it is either dreaming or contemplating the What? Why? and How? of Life.

If you feel that you are tired, then you are tired, if you think that you are old, you start feeling old; and if you are in the company of children, you feel young and energetic. Every human being likes to feel good, young, energetic and cheerful.

When we see an illiterate labourer toiling away on the roadside, we tend to think that he has to undergo these physical hardships because he either has no brain or whatever brain he has is very weak.

On the other hand, we think that a professionally qualified intellectual has a very big or sharp brain. If both the brains, that of the ignorant labourer and that of the intellectual, are analyzed by any Neurologist, it would be found that the size, volume and the structure of the brain cells are almost identical in both the brains!

The obvious question that then comes up is : If both brains are identical, then why is there such a big difference in the performance of the brains?

The answer to the question lies in the fact that there is a vast difference in the training of their respective 'MINDS'.

The labourer, due to adverse circumstances, is deprived

of the opportunity to obtain the right kind of stimulus for his mind and, as a consequence, the development of his mind and his thinking capacity is stinted.

On the other hand, the minds of the intellectuals (the Engineers, Architects, Doctors, Scientists, Scholars, Lawyers, Pilots, etc) are provided the appropriate stimuli right from the time of their birth through the formative years of their life. These stimuli help in developing the mind and they become experts in their chosen fields.

Similarly, we can train our minds to feel good, cheerful, young and disciplined at all times.

Five ways to balance the mind :

1.Silence :

Silence is very powerful. The Golden Rule is to speak less and listen more. God, while developing the prototypes of our bodies decided to give us one mouth and two ears. Why? So that we speak less and listen more! We must make it a habit to maintain silence (Maun) for a minimum of one hour everyday.

2.Meditation :

Meditation everyday morning and in the evening helps in controlling the mind and prevents it from wandering here and there. The human mind is similar to the hard disk of a Computer. When it gets overloaded with data, we have to delete some items, which have lost their utility. Similarly, when the mind is overloaded with feelings, emotions and thoughts, meditation helps us in purging the unwanted and unpleasant portions of our feelings, emotions and thoughts. This refreshes the mind and we are then able to think and see in a much brighter perspective.

3.Non - Judgment :

Do not judge any person or pass judgement unnecessarily in situations where it is unwarranted. Remember, when we point a finger at others, three fingers are pointing back at us!

4. Nature :

Spend time regularly in direct communion with nature. It not only enables us to sense the harmonious interaction of all the elements of nature and forces of life, but also gives us a sense of unity and love with all of life and develops the feeling of endless rhythm. Whether it be a stream, a forest, a mountain, a lake, a garden, the seashore or beautiful flowers, the communion with nature will also help you access the field of pure potentiality.

5.Innermost Essence :

We must learn to get in touch with the innermost essence of our being. This true essence is beyond the ego. It is fearless, it is free, it is immune to criticism, it does not fear any challenge, it is beneath no one, superior to no one, and full of magical mystery and enchantment.

Access to our essence will also give us insight into the mirror of relationship, because all relationships are a reflection of our own relationships with ourselves.

Just for example, if you have fear, guilt, or are feeling insecure financially or success, then these are reflections of fear, guilt or insecurity as basic aspects of your personality. No individual, or money or success will solve these basic problems of existence. Only intimacy with the self will bring about true healing.

When you really understand your true nature, you will never feel guilty or insecure, because you will realize that the essence of material wealth is life energy, it is pure potentiality, which is your intrinsic nature, your thought of mind.

As you gain more and more access to your true nature, you will also spontaneously receive creative thoughts with pure knowledge.

Always keep in mind that the five elements of nature and the beautiful things around you in the environment gives positive energy, color, heat, light, vegetable, trees, flowers etc. They exude positive energy very silently, without any ego.

For example, the Sun silently gives us light, color, heat, ultra violet rays and vitamins. 80% of life energy is given to us by the Sun.

The Earth silently provides us with all the basic raw material, minerals, green vegetables etc. It also gives us Spiritual, Divine, Medicinal and herbal plants, fruits and shaded trees. It silently gives mankind a range of life saving material without any discrimination of caste, creed and religion.

It is a misconception that 'Nature' is hostile to man. If approached in true harmony, its secrets can be revealed and the energies harnessed for the benefit of living beings.

Discover your divinity, find your unique talent, serve humanity with it, you can generate all the wealth that you desire make your life real before death.

When your creative mind matches the needs of your fellow humans, then wealth will spontaneously flow from the unmanifest into the manifest. You will begin to experience your life as a miraculous expression of divinity and you will know true joy and the art of blissful living.

Your very self is an ocean with a fortune of undiscovered wealth deep inside your mind, and unbounded love that you can offer to serve humanity.

Your ageless mind is so powerful that you can create any situation or any environment of your own choice around you.

The greatest discovery of mankind is that a human being can alter or mould his life by altering his attitude. That is the real successful **LIFE BEFORE BEATH**.

Accordingly the process of nature or cycle of life one gets moksha only after death.

Religion begins where science ends.

6

Life Before Death

History tells us about great ancient civilizations. Where have they gone? To museums, pyramids, history books, Discovery channel, etc? But Indian civilization, the ancient creed and culture, still are found in every village of India-alive and kicking!

The universal philosophy focuses on relation between God, Nature and Man, which overcomes all the barriers of diverse human-cultures. It leads to the highest level of self-realization, revealing the inner most secrets of the nature of self. All the aspects of life are integrated and taken in totality. Thus, rather than negation and or denial, it celebrates Life Before Death.

In the school of Indian philosophy which can inspire us for both material and spiritual progress.

I invite you to a blissful experience where you will explore the Inner Divinity and re-establish your joyous feeling of the Supreme unity of the self with the Universal Spirit. It will give you peace, happiness, good health and security. You will be able to extend harmony towards the outward environment.

This is an endeavourer of love with an invitation to the oriental wisdom and mystic knowledge. The purpose is to create a stir or motion of this beautiful creed and watch the feel uplifted. You can look forward to the future with hope and confidence.

This Vedic philosophy occupies a distinguished position among the various schools of spiritual thought and ideologies. This universal secular philosophy focuses on the relation between God, Nature and Man, which overcomes all the barriers of diverse human cultures. It leads to the highest level of self realization, revealing the innermost secrets of the nature of the self. All the aspects of life are integrated and taken in totality. Thus, rather than negation and denial, it celebrates life.

This Vedic Culture can inspire us for both material and spiritual progress. Rather, the approach is from theory to practice. Indeed, it leads us to the "Inner Bliss and Harmony".

The Research Institute of Vedic Culture (a N.G.O. Trust) programmer are aimed at the common man. While we remain busy with our routine and other work, we can be seekers and realize our goal of finding our Divine Natures. In this way, we are satisfied in our material and spiritual pursuits.

Please have a deep focus on the following three factors so that we are well oriented towards our goal. Kindly remember these three pillars.

1. **SUPREME UNITY OF THE SELF:** You are indeed a part of the great and most powerful Universal Spirit. Elevate yourself. Love and regard the Divinity in you. Have full faith in yourself. Similarly, discover the divinity in others. Oh! Everybody is a part of the supreme spirit. Let this vision totally influence us.

This outlook should guide our relationship and our thinking about others. Once again please remember you are part of the Supreme soul.

2. **TOTALITY OF HUMAN PERSONALITY:** I accept

you as are. Everybody has his own qualities, features, etc. You should appreciate this. The Almighty God has made everybody differently not even two flakes of snow are alike. So keeping this reality in mind, we have to start from where we are. We have to be content with all merits and demerits. We have no other place to go. Therefore, live and work in the present to be a true seeker.

3. **DIVINE GRACE:** "Knowledge is Bondage" - Vedic Culture. Please remember comprehension. We humans have a limited comprehension to seek Truth. That is why we are amazed at the happenings and we remark "Nothing is in our hands". Remember, all our efforts will bear fruit only by **His Grace**. Therefore, our efforts should be in harmony and focused towards this spirit. We will always gain in the process. So remember the path of realization through **Divine Grace**.

We aim at the transformation of common man or woman. We have deep faith in the spirituality of the common folk. So the idea is to have simple presentations, which will slowly carry us to the great heights and totally guide our lives. The programms consist of three stages.

1. **Prayer stage :** Indeed, prayers take us to the Inner Divinity and to our Lord! The invocation, chants, devotional prayers, mystic poetry, etc. work wonders on the human mind.

This is the best way to prepare for the spiritual path.

2. **Presentation stage :** This will focus on the knowledge of this blissful creed in slow and steady way so that it is possible to adopt it in our lives. We emphasize on the main concept of the Supreme Unity of the self. There will be inspiring stories with guidance, which is important to our life situations.

3. **Realization stage :** Here we address all the gross and subtle aspects of human development like Yoga for

body, Meditation for mind and Divine Grace for soul. We plan a systematic upward movement for the seeker leading to ultimate realization.

We emanate from Bliss, we sustain in Bliss and we merge in Bliss.

Summing up, you will experience a transformation in your life towards love, light and compassion with a perfect harmony in both material and spiritual aspects of life. Rather, the approach is from theory to practice. Indeed, it leads us to the real Art Of Blissful Living.

It is a matter of concern that nothing much is done in the land of discovery of Vedic philosophy. We should seriously ponder over this situation and consider the importance of Vedic philosophy in our present strife-torn world. A thrill of self confidence, the spirit of bliss, surpassing all barriers of caste, creed and gender, no look back, no regret, the inner journey, see everything as creation of God, etc, how prominently and conceptually these are emphasized in Vedic culture. It should be our solemn endeavour to present this ancient philosophy in common man's language so that resurgence takes place with the goal of Upliftment of an individual, society, nation and world as a whole.

As regards the Great Descend, Vedic Culture explains the process of cosmic evolution or universal experience, i.e., from God hood to veiling or obscuring force of nature called Maya Shakti leading to various psycho physical elements and finally the Panch Mahabhutas five great elements: Earth, Water, Fire, Air and Ether. (The Principal of Vastu Shastra also)

The first outward manifestation of the divine creative energy is called "Shiva Tattva". It is the initial creative movement of Paramasiva and is the support of all things in the manifest world, like the canvas of a painting. Next, the "Shakti- Tattava" is active or kinetic cosmic energy that effects the divine consciousness into action.

"Maya" is the ceiling or obscuring force of nature that creates a sense of differentiation. As such, it makes universal consciousness, which is unity, appear as duality and multiplicity. The results of the limitation of Maya are "Purusha" and "Prakriti", the limited being and his nature. Here the dual world of mind and matter is permanently established. This follows various mental operations, ascertaining intelligence, sense perceptions, ego etc. The process is completed finally with the gross Panch Mahabutas.

Now, let us consider the Ascend or going back to Godhood. What is source of pain and frustration- duality and moving away from God hood! So, it is natural that we must strive to go back to Godhood. For this there has to be Shaktipath- the descend of Divine Grace. In order to earn Grace, one has to undergo spiritual discipline, known as "Upyas" Yoga. Depending upon potential of an individual, these means or yoga have been categorized with particular emphasis as Anupaya(supreme means- Bliss), Shambopaya(higher means- Will), Shaktopaya(medium means- Knowledge) and Anvopaya(inferior means- Action). However, it must always be remembered that descend of the Divine Grace- Shaktipath- is independent of human efforts.

Vedic Culture emphasizes that one has to discover the inner "Bliss". Let us not suppress the senses; do not torture the body or mind, etc. Forcible control will lead to adverse effect. Be as you are. When one discovers inner bliss he/she will give up fascination for outer worldly enjoyments. Outwardly one may perform the age-old traditions but inwardly he/she has to seek exact truth through the practices taught in Yoga. There is no restriction based on colour, creed, gender, etc. in eligibility for initiation in Yoga.

As regards "Devotion", it is an essential aid to all the practices. An aspirant not blessed with devotion for the Lord cannot succeed in the practice or Saiva-yoga. After inculcating the principles and treading the path as explained above, we should surrender and submit to the Ultimate Reality. This will, no doubt, lead us to the ultimate Bliss.

This philosophy is very relevant for present times. It inspires us for both material and spiritual progress. It stresses positive acceptance of material world rather than the philosophy of escapism. Thus it can serve as a sound basis for organizing our lives. We can rather say that God has made man in his own image. It is His Own Maya Shakti, which makes man to see differently. Therefore, real joy can be gained as we live in this world and go about our work. Avoiding suppression and denial like great puritans, we should exercise moderation in living and turning away from the ambition of wealth, power and pleasures of senses. This will prepare us for the inward journey to realize God.

The youth should remember that no problem of individual, society or nation is to be ignored. A person cannot succeed in any aim of life if he shuts his eyes towards these problems. The whole life of Lord Krishna as depicted in Mahabharta is a glowing example of practical Shaivism.

We may enjoy tasteful worldly objects as per the tradition but consider or ponder over their origin from "the Divine Glory". This will enable us to look for God in every individual, see everything as His creation, etc., leading to maximum love and harmony.

Even as elderly persons we should be totally in world yet totally liberated from within. This example incorporated in our lives will definitely create an inspiration for others.

Summing up, let us work for upliftment as our goal. With our own effort we should change and strive for enlightenment. Let this change permeate from person to family, to state and nation as a whole. Leading to universal good this will usher in a peaceful and conflict free world.

7

Life After Death

Is there a LIFE AFTER DEATH ?, **Imagine** yourself, at a Darbar (Court of Justice) of the supreme God in Heaven. God asks you. "**What have you been doing on Earth Planet**"? Out of the thousand of Planets in the universe, I had sent you to the Earth Planet, where you had taken birth because of the existence of five Elements (Earth, Water, Fire, Air and Space) well balanced in your body. Hence you grow with the five senses (eyes, ears, nose, speech and touch) which I had bestowed upon you.

How best you utilized your wealth, knowledge and wisdom? Which I had been gifted to you, This will be another difficult question to answer after death. I am sure neither of us can escape to answer these questions nor can we hire any advocate or solicitor to represent our case.

These are the questions every body has to face and give answer after death. I wonder if we all have to face and give answer to these questions after death, Do we have any choice at the Darbar (Court of justice). Just imagine the situation. I don't think any one would want to be left blank and poker faced.

If we are convinced with the situation one has to face after death, can't we plan our behavior in advance with in this **Life Before Death**.

Yes the answer is very simple. With our "Karma" we can change our destiny. Whatever act we do, whatever our-behavior is in our society, we live with our family. How we possess our wealth and knowledge, and how we spend or share it, that is our Karma.

What is Karma?

As explained in Bhagavad-Gita Lord Krishana telling Arjuna do your duties (Karma) by using your five senses through knowledge. The knowledge comes from Vedas.

Once we are sure we have to stand trial (after death) in the court of Almighty, we should prepare our self accordingly. We should be very careful of our actions and behavior towards our family and society. We should share our wealth and knowledge with others and spread the message of the God, Lord Krishna has very clearly defined "Karma" in Bhagavad Gita. He tells Arjuna that one should always do his duties (karmas) sincerely by using the five senses and developing them through knowledge and the knowledge comes from Vedas only.

What is Karma yoga?

Everybody is engaged in some sort of activity in this material world. But one's actions can either bind him to this world or liberate him from it. By acting for the pleasure of the supreme, without selfish motives, one can be liberated from the law of karma (action and reaction) and attain **Transcendental Knowledge** of the self and the supreme.

What is TRANSCENDENTAL KNOWLEDGE?

Transcendental knowledge is the spiritual knowledge of the soul, of the God, and of their fruit of selfless devotional action (karma yoga). The Lord explains the remote history of the Bhagavad Gita, the purpose and significance of his periodic descents to the material world, and the necessity of approaching a guru (a realized teacher).

The ultimate purpose of Vedic knowledge is to detach one self from the entanglement of the material world and to understand the **Supreme Personality**, one who understands the difference between the body, the soul and the super soul (The Supreme Personality) beyond them both attains liberation from this material world.

Sanskrit Shloka

Arjuna uvaca prakrtim pursam caiva kawrem ksetrajnam eva ca
etad veditum icchami jnanam jneyam ca kesava
sri bhagavan uvaca
idam sariram kaunteya ksetram ity abhidhiyate etad yo vetti tam prahuh
ksetrajnah iti tad-vidah

Gita. 13.1

Meaning: Arjuna said: Oh my dear Krishna, I wish to know about prakrti [nature], Purusa [the enjoyer], and the field and the knower of the field, and of knowledge and the object of knowledge. The Blessed Lord then said:
This body, Oh son of Kunti, is called the field, and one who knows this body is called the knower of the field.

It is not very difficult to understand the difference between the field and its knower, the body and the knower of the body. Any person can visualize that from childhood to old age as he undergoes so many changes in his body and still remains one person. There is a difference between the knower of the field of activities and the actual field of activities. In a living conditioned soul can understand that he is different from the body.

Sanskrit Shloka:

Ksetrajnam capi mam viddhi sarva-ksetresu bharata
ksetra-ksetrajnayor jnanam yat taj jnanam matam mama

Gita 13.3

Meaning: O scion of Bharata, you should understand that I am also the knower in all bodies, and to understand this body and its owner is called knowledge. That is my opinion.

While discussing the subject of this body and the owner of the body, the soul and the Super-soul, we shall find three different topics of study: the Lord, the living entity, and matter. In every field of activities, in every body, there are two souls: the individual soul and the super-soul.

Because the Super-soul is the planetary expansion of the Supreme Personality of Godhead, Krishna says, "I am also the knower, but I am not the individual owner of the body. I am the super-knower. I am present in every body as the Paramatma, or Super-soul.

Sanskrit Shloka: -

Maha-bhutany ahankaro buddhir avyaktam eva ca
Indriyani dasaikam ca panca cendriya-gocarah
Iccha dvesah sukham duhkham sanghatas cetana dhrtih
etat ksetram samasena sa-vikaram udahrtam

Gita. 13. 6 & 7.

Meaning: The five great elements, false ego, intelligence, the unmanifested, the ten senses, the mind, the five sense objects, desire, hatred, happiness, distress, the aggregate, the life symptoms, and convictions all these are considered, in summary, to be the field of activities and its interactions.

Seen from all the authoritative statements of the great sages, the Vedic hymns and the aphorisms of the Vedanta-sutra, the components of this world are earth, water, fire, air and space. These are the five great elements (mahabhuta). Then there is false ego, intelligence and the unmanifested stage of the three modes of nature.

There are five senses for acquiring knowledge: the

eyes, ears, nose, tongue and touch. The five working senses: voice, legs, hands, the anus and the genitals. Above these senses, there is the mind, which controls the whole body.

Therefore, including the mind, there are eleven senses and the object of these senses are smell, taste, warmth, touch and sound. "

Now the aggregate of these twenty-four elements is called the field of activity. If one makes an analytical study of these twenty-four subjects, then he can very well understand the field of activity. Then there is desire, hatred, pleasure and pain, which are interactions, representations of the five great elements in the gross body.

The living symptoms, represented by consciousness and conviction, are the manifestation of the subtle body-mind, ego and intelligence. These subtle elements are included within the field of activities.

The five great elements are a gross representation of the subtle false ego. They are a representation in the material conception. Consciousness is represented by intelligence, of which the unmanifested stage is the three modes of material nature. The unmanifested three modes of material nature is called pradhana.

One who desires to know the twenty-four elements in detail along with their interactions should study the philosophy of Bhagavad - Gita.

To keep the total balance of combination "Man, Material and Nature" in relation with five elements.

The body is the representation of all these factors. There are changes of the body, which are six in number: the body is born, it grows, it stays, it produces by-products, then begins to decay, and at the last stage it vanishes. Therefore, the field is a nonpermanent material thing.

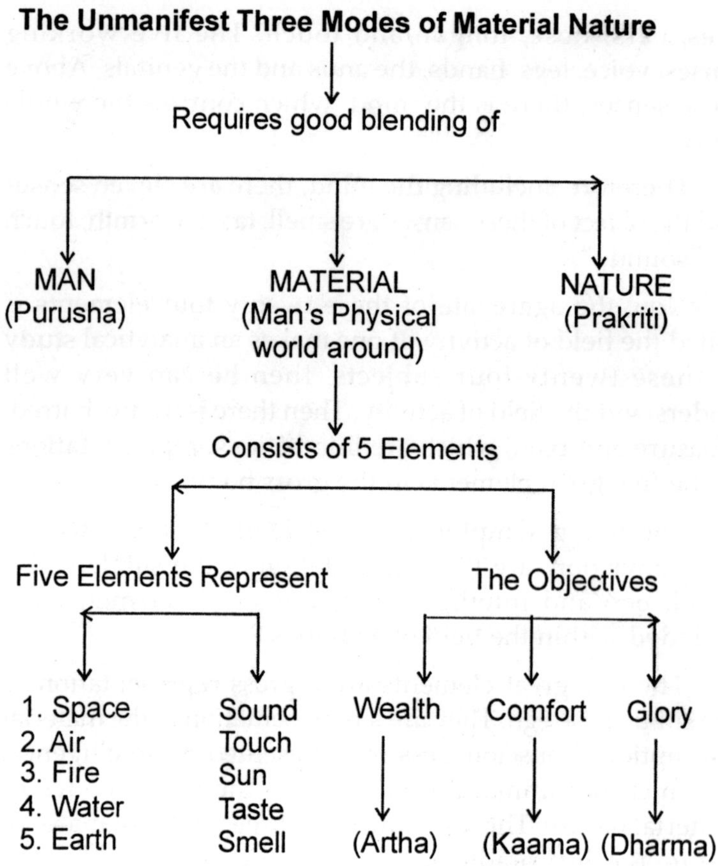

Sanskrit Shloka: -

Amanitvam adambhitvam ahimsa ksantir arjavam
acaryopasanam saucam sthairyam atma- vinigrahah
indriyarthesu vairaagyam anhankara eva ca
janma-mrtyu-jara-vyadhi-duhkha-dosanudarsanam
asaktir anabhisvangah putra-dara-grhadisu
nityam ca sama-cittatvam istanistopapattisu
mayi cananya yogena bhaktir avyabhicarini
vivikta-desa-sevitvam aratir jana-samsadi
adhyatma-jnana-nityatvam tattva-jnanartha-
darsanam

etaj jnanam iti proktam ajanam yad ato'nyatha

Gita 13.12

Meaning : Humility, prayerlessness, nonviolence, tolerance, simplicity, approaching a bonafide spiritual master, cleanliness, steadiness and self-control; renunciation of the objects of sense gratification, absence of false ego, the perception of the evil of birth, death, old age and disease; non attachment to children, wife, home and the rest, and even-mindedness a mid pleasant and unpleasant events; constant and unalloyed devotion to Me, resorting to solitary places, detachment from the general mass of people; accepting the importance of self-realization, and philosophical search for the Absolute Truthall these I thus declare to be knowledge, and what is contrary to these is ignorance.

CONSCIOUSNESS

What is more important ? Gyan or Vigyan (knowledge or science), In the school and colleges the student only get certificates and degrees. The knowledge comes from the spiritual master.

"I was born in the darkest ignorance, and my spiritual master opened my eyes with the touch of knowledge"

A broad based education really means that the students are prepared for life, without losing their areas of specialization or competence.

An expert is someone who knows all the answers if you ask the right questions.

Education and knowledge, without commonsense, has little meaning. Commonsense is the ability to see things as they are, and do them, as they ought to be done.

We are born with five senses (touch, taste, sight, smell,

and hearing). But successful people have a sixth sense called commonsense; commonsense is gained in spite of, not necessarily as a result of, education. The best education without commonsense is worthless. Continuous positive education leads to positive thinking.

Learning is like eating food everyday. It is not important how much you eat; what counts is how much you digest.

This process of knowledge is sometimes misunderstood by less intelligent men as being the interaction of the field of activity. But actually this is the real process of knowledge. If one accepts this process, then the possibility of approaching the Absolute Truth exists. This is not the interaction of the tenfold elements, as described before; this is actually the means to get out of it, all the descriptions of the process of knowledge.

As for the knowledge outlined here, the items may be analyzed as follows: Humility means that one should not be anxious to have the satisfaction of being honored by others. The material conception of life makes us very eager to receive honor from others, but from the point of view of a man, in perfect state of knowledge, who knows that he is not this body, anything, honor or dishonor, pertaining to his body is useless. One should not be hankering after this material deception.

People are very anxious to be famous for their religion, and consequently sometimes it is found that without understanding the principles of religion, one enters into some group, which is not actually following religious principles. Then he wants to advertise himself as a religious mentor. But for actual advancement in spiritual science, one should have a test to see how far he is progressing. He can judge by these items.

Nonviolence is generally taken to mean not killing or destroying the body; but actually nonviolence means not to put others into distress. People in general are trapped by ignorance in the material concept of life, and they perpetually suffer material pains. So, unless one elevates people to spiritual knowledge, one is practicing violence.

One should try his best to distribute real knowledge to the people, so that they may become enlightened and leave this material entanglement. That is **nonviolence**.

Tolerance means that one should be prepared for daily life practice, to bear, insult and dishonor from others. If one is engaged in the advancement of spiritual knowledge, there will be so many insults and much dishonor from others. This is expected, because material nature is so constituted.

Even a boy like Prahlada, who, was five years old, who was engaged in the cultivation of spiritual knowledge, was endangered when his father became antagonistic towards his devotion. The father tried to kill him in so many ways, but Prahlada tolerated him.

So, for making advancement in spiritual knowledge, there may be many impediments; but we should be tolerant and continue our progress with determination; particularly, in this modern age.

Simplicity means that without diplomacy one should be completely straightforward. As for acceptance of the spiritual master, that is essential, because without the instruction of a bona fide spiritual master, one cannot progress in the spiritual science.

One should approach the spiritual master with all humility and offer him all services so that he will be pleased to bestow his blessings upon the disciple.

If he bestows any blessings upon his disciple that will make the disciple immediately advance without the disciple having to follow the regulated principles. Or, the regulated principles will be easier for one who has served the spiritual master without reservation.

Cleanliness is essential for making advancement in spiritual life. There are two kinds of cleanliness: external and internal. External cleanliness means taking a bath, but for internal cleanliness, one has to think of God, and speak truth.

False ego means accepting this body as oneself. When one understands that he is not his body and is spirit soul that is real ego. Ego is there. False ego is condemned, but not real ego. In the Vedic literature, it is said: aham brahmasmi. I am Brahman, I am spirit. This "I am," the sense of self, also exists in the liberated stage of self-realization. This sense of "I am" is ego, but when the sense of " I am" is applied to this false body, it is false ego. When the sense of self is applied to reality that is real ego.

There are some philosophers who say we should give up our ego, but we cannot give up our ego because ego means identity. We ought, of course, to give up the false identification with the body.

One should try to understand the distress of **accepting birth, death, old age and disease**. There are descriptions in various Vedic literatures of birth. In the Srunad-Bhagavatam the world of the unborn, the child's stay in the womb of the mother, its suffering, etc., are all very graphically described. It should be thoroughly understood that birth is distressful.

Because we forget how much distress we suffer within the womb of the mother, we do not make any solution to the repetition of **birth and death**.

Similarly at the time of death, there are all kinds of sufferings, and they are also mentioned in the authoritative scriptures. These should be discussed. And as far as disease and old age are concerned, everyone gets practical experience. No one wants to be diseased, and no one wants to become old, but we cannot avoid these. Unless we have a pessimistic view of this material life, considering the distresses of birth, death, old age and disease, there is no impetus for our making advancement in spiritual life.

As for detachment from children, wife and home, it is not meant that one should have no feeling for them. They are natural objects of affection, but when they are not favorable to spiritual progress then one should not be attached to them. The best process for making the home pleasant is self-God consciousness.

Count your blessing, not your troubles. Find time to smell the roses and enjoy the beauty of colours. Don't count the thorns.

I ask you not to cry over spilt milk (The Past). It spoils our present and we also fear the future that is concealed from us by providence. Why probe into what God chooses to hide from us? You thereby create suffering for yourself. Forget the past, keep the gate shut behind you and hold no anxiety about the future. **Live in the 'Present'** for it is the only moment you have.

It is rightly said:

- The PAST is History
- The FUTURE is a mystery
- The PRESENT is just what it is, A GIFT, make the best of it!
- Listen to your body's wisdom, the signals of comfort and discomfort.
- Take time to be silent, to meditate, to silence the internal dialogue.
- My happiness depends upon the way I meet the events of life, not on the events.
- Real renunciation is giving up that which the mind likes the most.
- No expectations means no disappointments.
- Want makes us a beggar. Everything comes unto him who dies not desire or care for anything.

- Be content with whatever you do, without attachment or sense of desire.
- He is a brave man who can say 'no'. Desire is increased by desire.
- When we feel and accept God's will at all times, how can we want anything?
- I possess nothing, therefore I renounce nothing - I want nothing, as I am everything.
- Neither seek nor avoid, take what comes; this is contentment.
- When you accept life, life accepts you. Allow your nature to carry out the will of higher power.
- You cannot buy bliss with money.
- One who possesses is possessed; one who is contented is liberated.
- Love bestows upon the receiver but gives to the giver too. Be not miserly in love.
- Love knows no bargaining, asks nothing but gives everything in which individuality vanishes and there is communion.
- If you decide to love a person even with his faults, then it is not chance, it's your choice.
- We waste time looking for the perfect lover, instead of creating the perfect love.
- Love is not an action but a state of mind.
- Love is the master key to open door of liberation.
- Love is the saviour of Life; it bestows supreme peace and everlasting joy.
- Have an encouraging, positive, cheerful, hopeful and loving attitude.
- It is good to forgive but best is to forget.
- Man is ever in Debt for the welfare given to him and therefore can have no claim or demand on anyone.

- Our life is what our thoughts make it.
- Man can work his own miracles, provided he has faith, conviction and equanimity.
- Fame is a communicable disease.
- Your goal is to discover infinity worth in yourself.
- Every situation in life will change. Favorable and unfavorable times will come and go. Therefore, do not seek God's blessing for objects.
- A true seeker never expects God to alter or change his situation as predicaments come according to one's own destiny and deeds.
- Have faith and Shradha in yourself. Ignite the light of wisdom within. Surrender yourself to God without any ego, cleverness or shrewdness.
- Don't try to change people, accept them as they are.
- If you are changed, the whole world is changed for you.
- Impartial justice is the greatest mercy of God.
- God gives what you need and not what you want or desire.
- Relinquish your need for external approval; you alone are the judge of your worth.
- Believe and trust in the Goodness and caring power of God. Thy 'will' be done.
- Count your blessing and be grateful to the Almighty.
- Confession is a virtue of few.
- When you are in anger or opposition with circumstances, realize that you are struggling within yourself.
- When you relinquish your anger, you will be healing yourself and co-operating with the flow of the Universe.
- I want to be happy; but I can be happy only if I make others happy.
- Devotion to God increases in the same proportion as attachment to the objects of the senses decreases.
- Keep yourself busy; you will have no time for worrying.

- Be clean, not clever. See no evil in others.
- Life is a challenge – Meet it.
- Life is a gift – Accept it.
- Life is a sorrow – Overcome it.
- Life is a duty – Perform it.
- Life is a game – Play it.
- Life is a song – Sing it.
- Life is a promise – Fulfill it.
- Life is a love – Enjoy it.
- Life is a smile – Give it to others.
- Life is an experience – Share it with others.
- Life is knowledge – Distribute it.
- Life is a charity – Donate it.

The most fortunate happening of my existence is that I have been born as a "Human Being" with superior faculties, to ensure that the human body so awarded, is properly maintained.

If you find some one who has lost his smile, kindly give yours.

Do not go into the history of God, but go into his mystery and try to learn the Vedic Gyan yog (knowledge), know the truth shall make you free from fearlessness and purify your mind, body and soul.

Sanskrit Shloka:

Sri bhagavan uvaca abhayam sattva-amsuddhir
jnan-yoga-vyavasthitih danam damas ca yajnas ca
svadhyayas tapa arjavam
Ahimsa satyam akrodhas tyagah santir apaisunam
daya bhutesv aloluptvam mardavam hrir acapalam
tejah ksama dhrtih saucam adroho natimanita
bhavanti sampadam daivim abhijatasya bharata

Gita 16.3

Meaning : The blessed Lord said: Fearlessness, purification of one's existence, cultivation of spiritual knowledge, charity, self-control, performance of sacrifice, study of the Vedas, austerity and simplicity; nonviolence, truthfulness, freedom from anger; renunciation, tranquility, aversion to faultfinding, compassion and freedom from covetousness; gentleness, modesty and steady determination; vigor, forgiveness, cleanliness, freedom from envy and the passion for honor-these transcendental qualities, O son of Bharata, belong to godly men endowed with divine nature.

Sanskrit Shloka:

Karmany evadhikaras te ma phalesu kadacana
ma karma-phala-hetur bhur ma te sango'stv akarmani

Gita. 2.47

Meaning : You have a right to perform your prescribed duty, but you are not entitled to the fruits of action. Never consider yourself to be the cause of the results of your activities and never be attached to not doing your duty.

There are three considerations here; prescribed duties, capricious work, and inaction. Prescribed duties refer to activities performed while one is in the modes of material nature. Capricious work means actions without the sanction of authority, and inaction means not performing one's prescribed duties.

One should not be inactive, but that he performs his prescribed duty without being attached to the result. One who is attached to the result of his work is also the cause of the action. Thus he is the enjoyer or sufferer of the result of .such actions.

Sanskrit Shloka:

Buddhi- yukto jahatiha ubhe sukrta-duskrte
tasmad yogaya yujuasva yogah karmasu kausalam

Gita. 2. 50

> **Meaning :** A man engaged in devotional service rids himself of both good and bad actions even in this life. Therefore strive for yoga, O Arjuna, which is the art of all work.

In this way one become free from the cycle of birth and death and attain the state beyond all miseries.

8

Importance of Traditional Chanting of Vedic Mantras

According to Indian tradition, Veda is the primeval speech of creation and the earliest literary records of ancient Indian Civilization. Modern scholars also accept that Rigveda is the earliest book of this world and bears immense value of Indian cultural tradition. Hence, to understand the earliest nature of human beings and their values and to investigate the developmental process of the same, the preservation and contemplation of the Vedas are most essential.

Being the fountainhead of all cultures, the Veda has to be preserved and studied for understanding the history, culture and linguistic analysis of human being. It is the foundation and treasure of various studies, like- science, metaphysics, philosophy and allied subjects.

All the Vedas have upavedas or secondary knowledge, viz. the Ayurveda or science of medicine of the Rigveda, Dhanurveda or science of archery of Yajurveda, the Gandharvaveda or science of music of the Samaveda and the Sthapatyaveda or architecture of the Atharvaveda, Vastu Shastra. (Ref, my books Vedic Architecture & Art of Living, (2nd) Vastu Science for 21st century and (3rd) The Art of Blissful Living.)

UNESCO, a world cultural organization, is now trying to enliven this oral tradition of the Vedas and Vedic heritage for preservation and promotion of the multifarious scientific and earliest oral tradition of chanting Veda mantras.

Vedic texts are classified mainly into four groups Rk, Yahus, Saman and Atharvan. Each of them has different recensions (sakhas), of which many have become extinct and only a few exist now. At the time of Patanjali, Rigveda had 21 recensions, Sukla-Yajurveda had 9- in total 1131recensions. But at present, only 13 recensions exist. Of these Rigveda has 2, Sukla-Yajurveda 2, Krsna-Yajurveda 4, Samaveda 3 and Atharvaveda only 2. Among these recensions, some oral traditions are also lost and only 8 to 10 octogenarian Vedic scholars of some recensions are known throughout India.

Seven musical notes of the Samaveda sadja, rsabha, gandhara, madhyama, pancama, dhaivata, and nisada, remain latent in other Vedas among the three accents- udatta (acute), anudatta (grave) and svarita (circumflex) in different way.

There, nisada and gandhara are latent in udatta, rsabha and dhaivata are in anudatta and sadja, madhyama and pancama are in svarita. It may be noted that the Gandharvaveda or science of music evolved from the Samaveda. This Samavedic chanting tradition has to be preserved properly as it is the source of Indian music.

In the field of performing arts like drama etc. four Vedas are connected vividly as recitation (pathya) from the Rigveda, music (gita) from the Samaveda, acting (abhinaya) from the Yajurveda and aesthetic sentiment (rasa) from the Atharvaveda.

Vedas are the reflection of the original ultimate sound, which is eternal, all pervading and non-destructible. Importance of Vedic mantras lies not only in their meaning, but also in the sound through accurate chanting by respective oral tradition with proper accent (svara-prkriya), like udatta, anudatta and svarita, etc. The correct pronunciation of each Vedic syllable or letter along with the proper accents is absolutely essential. The hastamudras (hand postures) used while chanting the hyms, particularly, of the Sukla- Yajurveda impart a mystic effect.

Sound of Vedic mantras reach to our ears in two ways: - (i) as vibration of ether and (ii) as vibration of air. Vibration of ether cannot be perceived in the physical sense.

It is only a matter of realization and a result of internal vibration in the body of a seer belonging to para, pasyanti and madhyama stages bearing the un-struck sound (anahata-nada).

The second kind of sound is produced for certain vibration in the air reflecting an image of ethereal vibration.

It is audible and is realized not only by the chanter of Vedic mantras at the vaikhari stage resulting a struck sound (ahata-nada), but also by the listeners or audience of the same due to the eternal vibrative power of throbbing in chanting with minute and rapid vibrations in pitch as prescribed by the respective Vedic tradition. As in Tantric puja ritual, nyasa, the sequential placement of the letters of Sanskrit alphabet on the worshipper's body acts as a tool for the transformation of consciousness through the eternal power of sound, in the same way, the pronunciation of Vedic syllables in proper place of articulation gives a healing power to Vedic chanter and audience. Besides, the resonance of the Vedic notation sanctifies the place and environment.

In order to keep the Vedic mantras unchanged from time immemorial, the Vedic teachers suggested various modes of svadhyayas or daily chanting of the Vedas. Among these various modes, three are taken as original pathas (prakrti patha) samhitapatha, padapatha and kramapatha. Samhitapatha means continuous recitation of separate words joined together according to some rules of euphonic combination, while padpatha means a process of chanting the Vedic words with a clear separation from each other.

In Kramapatha, a sequential order and the accents of words are intact and to learn the Vedas by heart. They also started to chant the Vedas in reverse and repetitive orders known as vikrtipatha with its eight sub-varieties, viz. jata, mala, sikha, rekha, dhvaja, danda, ratha and ghana. Due to these vikrtipathas or chanting in different ways, the Vedic mantras remain unchanged and not a single letter if word is lost.

Varnakrama is also an important factor in Vedic chanting, especially in the Krsna-Yajurveda tradition where the knowledge of dhvani (sound), sthana (place of articulation), karana (means or instrument), prayatnai (effort), kala (time), devata (deity) and jata (genus) of each letter is shown. (Ref. My book Ageless Mind and The Art of Blissful Living)

9

The Role of Vedic Culture to Enjoy Beneficial Living

Vedic Philosophy

The aim of Vedic Philosophy is to first discover the secret laws of the Universe and then from them shape a pattern to be used for every day life.

I have attempted to take a microscopic section from the magnificent Vedic period to discover the scientific reason to show how close the people are to nature, and thereby learn the art of meaningful and beneficial living.

To achieve the desired benefit in true spirit, let us distinguish clearly the known from the unknown.

The Mystery of the Unknown is the essence of all activities of human achievements. The Unknown truth is always a concept, it can only be realized by the soul, it cannot be materialized, because it vanishes the moment you reach the point. Every 'CREATION' emerges from the Unknown which was there from the beginning of all the beginnings.

Sanskrit Shloka: -

AUM Purnamadah Purnamidam Purnat Purnam Udachyate PurnasyaPurnmadaya Purnameva Vashishyate

Meaning : This is perfect, that is perfect and from the perfect the perfect emerges. If perfect is deducted from the perfect only the perfect remains.

The Vedantic learning process insists on constantly reminding us of the following principles in the form of peace invocation chanted before starting every lesson.

Sanskrit Shloka:

Sehnavavtu Sehnobhunaktu Sehviryam Keravavahai,
TejasvinaWadhitamastu Ma Vidvishavahai,
AUM Shanti Shanti Shanti

Meaning : Let him protect us both, we be blessed with the bliss of knowledge, Let us do the brave act together 'May our studies be thorough and faithful, May we never misunderstand each other, Oh Eternity, Peace, Peace, Peace.

To get a perfect result it is always important to put a correct question than to give a correct answer to a wrong question.

THE RUDIMENTS OF VEDANTIC THOUGHTS

Nature has always been kind to man. If approached in true harmony nature's secrets can be revealed and its energies harnessed for the benefit of all living beings. Nature, Man and Product are all within the evolutionary network guided by our Karmas. **Vastu Shastra** A Vedic Architectural beauty is to be seen, felt, perceived, conceived and experienced.

While the present western generation is looking to the materialistic world for desired peace of mind and happiness, an open secret is relatively unknown that India is the fountainhead of the vast ancient Vedic knowledge, which is the source of everlasting peace, bliss and joy. When the Vedic concept is presented through modern technological advances, the sublime information becomes available which can be easily understood.

In the Vedic period, people build homes and hermitages with a view to have a peaceful life, offered prayers to live in Universal harmony.

But, in the modern world, people build concrete clusters of buildings mainly for a high rate of return, which has resulted in worldwide pollution, environmental and ecological problems, with no peace of mind.

The Vedic concept was derived with a view to help mankind live in peace, harmony and happiness on this planet.

Sanskrit Shloka:

> Serve Bhavantu Sukhinah Serve Santu Niramaya,
> Serve Bhadrani Pashyantu Ma Kaschid dukhbhagbhavet.
>
> **Meaning :** May all be happy. May all be free from disabilities, May all look to the good of others, May none suffer from sorrow. Let the whole world be in peace and prosperity.

One ponders to find answers to vital questions like:

- How did the Universe evolve?
- What is the real constitution of a human being?
- What is the Ultimate? Etc.

The Vedas Proclaim that the Divine Consciousness is without beginning or end, it is Omnipresent and the Omnipotent and Omniscient.

The "Eternal" contains:

- Space (Akash)
- Time (Kaal)
- Energy (Prana)
- Nature (Prakriti)

This all-pervading consciousness regulates the entire Cosmos and gives a spark of life to all individual beings.

The Cycle of Life

The distinction between the eternal spirit, the soul and the changing material body: As the embodied soul continually passes into material body from childhood to youth to old age, the soul similarly passes into astral body at death. The material body merges with the five elements of nature.

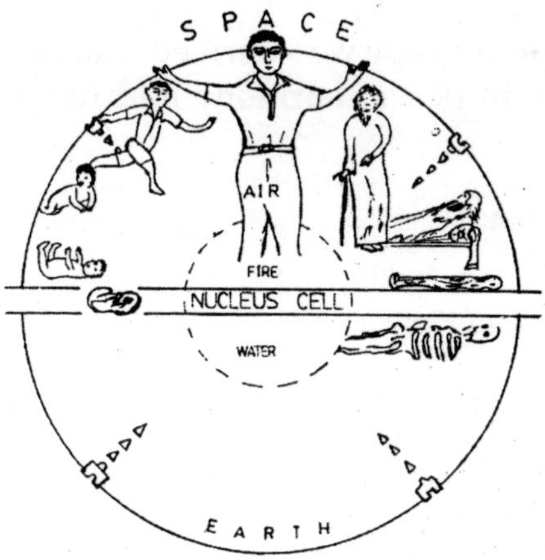

THE CYCLE OF LIFE

Diag. 9.1

The Vedas Say:

- There are laws of creation
- The law of maintenance and evolution.
- The law of dissolution.

The rudiments of Vedantic thoughts can be depicted in Trimurti.

Brahma The Creator
Vishnu The Sustainer
Mahesh The Annihilator

The Universe is governed by the innumerable laws, which are always in state of Evolution. THE MAN is the only creature who is blessed with the power of the MIND, which is the unique creation of the great Designer.

Diag. 9.2

To enjoy this grand play of consciousness, the Leela of Purusha and Prakriti, one has to:

- Observe it
- Discover it
- Enjoy it
- Create out of it and merge into it again.

A Three-Letter Mahamantra "AUM" The symbol of the divinity that pervades the Universe.

The first sound vibration of the Universe was "AUM".

The Mahamantra "AUM" represents the eternal endlessness of the Universe (time & space) and so endlessness of knowledge and information.

The " AUM " is the healing mantra predicting:

Satt (Truth)

Chit (Mind)

Anand (Happiness)

In regular meditation and Japa, AUM produces such an enormous and powerful vibration that it virtually gives emergence to the five elements (Space, Air, Fire, Water &

Earth) of which, the entire Srishti the Universe is composed of.

Diag. 9.3 : OM

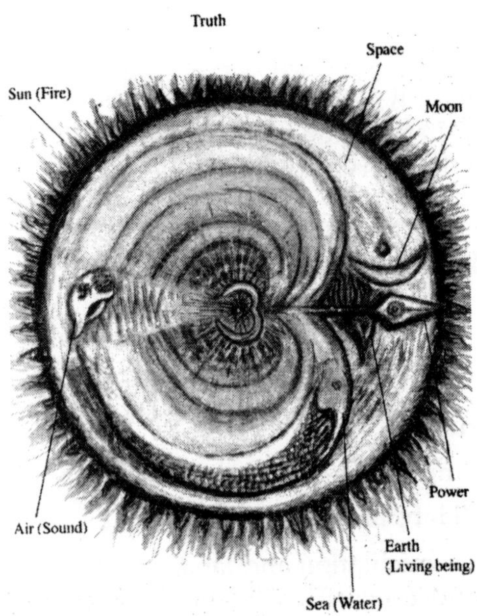

Diag. 9.4

What are Vedas?

The Vedas are a systematic and formulated source of knowledge that explains the relationship between Man, Nature and God.

The Vedas train us to think for ourselves and to rediscover one-self, to analyze, investigate and realize the very essence of life. Living a contented life is an art, a skill, a technique which all of us need to learn and master to achieve mental peace and harmony.

The Vedas offer us a practical way of life, which satisfies our Spiritual need, and gives mental peace along with material prosperity.

Your very self is an ocean with a fortune of undiscovered wealth deep inside you and the unbounded love that you can offer to others. Your mind is so powerful that you can create an environment of your own choice around you.

Let us all be true seekers and devote ourselves to reach the state of ultimate bliss and liberation

The Science and Philosophy of the Vedas is the answer to the all the needs of mankind.

In order to seek the scientific answers to all questions and to understand the role of Vedic culture in our modern day to day living, our Rishis and Munis who had a deep knowledge of the laws of nature developed a number of scientific systems which are explained in the Vedas. Some of them are as given below: -

Vastu Shastra:

Vastu Kala, Vastu Manav Shilpa, Vastu Shilpa Shastra, Vastu Deva Shilpa, Vastu Science & the Five elements of Nature.

Health & Spirituality, Meditation & Yoga, Ayurveda, Vedic, Herbal, Divine & Spiritual Plants,

Vedas & Himalayan Eco System, Mantra, Yantra, Prayer & Spiritual Healing.

Sanskrit Shloka:

" Na pranena na apranena martyo jivati Kaschana,
Itarena tu jivanti yasmin etavapasritau."

Meaning : Our life does not depend merely on the breathing process. The intake of food, which are indeed important for the body, but health, does not rest on food alone, because everything can be thrown out of order if the mind is upset.

A turbulence injected into the mind is enough to disturb the entire balance of personality.

Our Consciousness comprises of three stages of awareness: -

Waking, Dreaming & Deep sleep

We also have three behavioral qualities:

'Satvic', 'Rajasic' and 'Tamasic': Spiritual, psychological or merely lethargic ways of living. We are taught that by knowledge, selfless service and by meditation we can achieve the ultimate.

- Knowledge can be derived from 'Yantras'
- Creativity from 'Tantras'
- Energies from 'Mantras'
- Inspiration from 'Meditation'

I have combined all these together in my practice of Vastu to achieve best results. This would give a new outlook to the world of Vedic architecture, based on Vastu Shastra and Vedic Culture.

The Total Man: If Man is the reflection of Nature, Vedas reflect Man and his total personality. Human body and mind are complex instruments, which communicate, absorb, expand and get consumed in the nature. (Man,

Vedas and Nature are the natural evolutionary extensions of one another, forming a complete whole.)

These Symbols represent

Space - Sound

Air - Touch

Fire - Sun

Water - Taste

Earth - Smell

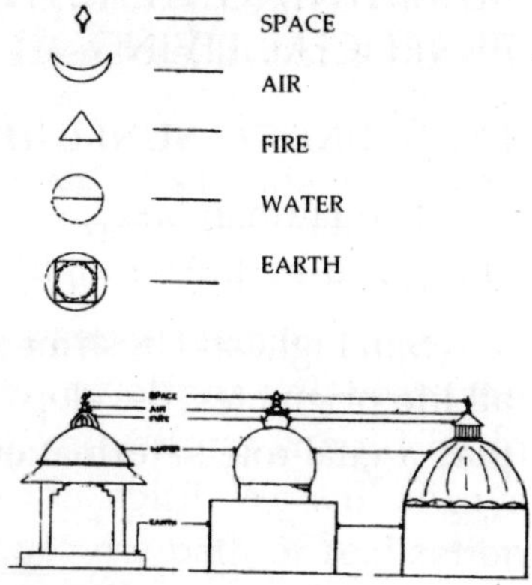

Diag. 9.5

OUR ATTITUDE TOWARDS THE VEDAS

These days the entire world is seriously concerned about the ecological imbalance, environment and pollution. But, our Rishis and Munis have given us these mantras thousands of years in advance.

Shanti Path:

> **The Vedas Say :**
> AUM Dyau Shanti Antakrish gvam, Shanti Prithvi, Shanti Rapah, Shanti Roshadhaya, Shanti Vanspatya, Shanti Vishvedavah, Shanti Brahma, Shanti Servagyum, Shanti Shanti Revah, Shanti Sa Ma, Shanti Redhi, AUM Shanti Shanti Shanti AUM ll
>
> **Meaning :** The peace that resides in the environment, in Solar World, in Space, in the Earth and Five Elements Water, nourishes the herbs, fruits and grains thereby nourishing the original power in all beings. May the peace of the world

now and forever come into us, we pray, May the highest good prevail.

COSMIC ENERGY FROM SUN, AIR, LIGHT & COLOR BALANCES MAN, MATERIAL & NATURE FOR SUSTAINING HEALTH & HAPPINESS TO ENJOY BENEFICIAL LIVING

EXPOSURE TO SUNLIGHT

The Human body, is truly a living photocell, which is energized by the Sunlight.

Sun Light and fresh air are the basic elements from which all life originates, develops, heals and evolves light and air play a vital role in formation of principles of Vastu Shastra.

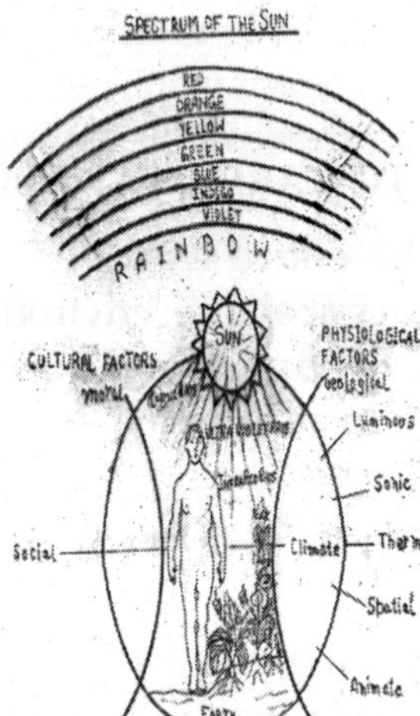

Human Comfort Level

Diag 9.6 : HUMAN HEALTH & LONGEVITY LEVEL

Sanskrit Shloka:-

Dhaunch ma Idam Prithvi Chantariksh cha me Vyachaha
Agnihi Surya aapo Medham Vishve Devascha Sam Dadhu

(Atharva Ved 12/1/53)

Heaven, Sun, Earth and fresh Air
Have given me this wide space,
And all Cosmic Powers
Together have endowed me with the Intellect.
(Atharva Ved 12/1/53)

Benefits of Exposure to Morning Sunlight

- Produces Vitamin D in the body resulting in normal growth and development of bones.
- Decreases Blood Sugar
- Balances Blood Pressure
- Decreases resting heart rate
- Decreases respiratory rate
- Decreases Lactic Acid in blood
- Increases resistance to Arthritis

Scientific Evidence:

ULTRA VIOLET LIGHT (UV Light) is an effective treatment for many diseases. The Sun Therapy is very commonly used in Naturopathy and is included in treatment of anemia, gout, colitis, cystitis, arthritis, eczema, acne, herpes, lupus, sciatica, asthma, kidney problems and even burns.

UV Light increases the efficiency of the heart: At the Tulane School of Medicine, Dr. Raymond Johnson exposed 20 people to Ultra Violet Light. In 18 out of 20 people their cardiac output increased an average of 39%. In other words, their hearts became stronger and pumped more blood.

UV Light is an effective treatment for Psoriasis : Reports from the National Psoriasis Foundation indicate that 80% of those suffering from this skin disease improve when they are exposed to UV Light.

UV Light activates the synthesis of Vitamin D: Dr. Robert Neer and his associate scientists conducted a study on a group of elderly persons to determine if extra sunlight would increase their ability to absorb calcium from their diets. The group which did not receive UV rays had 25% decrease in Calcium absorption while the other group receiving UV Rays had a 15% increase in absorption.

UV Light increases the level of sex hormones: In a study at Boston State Hospital, Dr. Abraham Myerson found that ultra violet light increased male hormones level by 120% and activates Melatonin a skin hormone.

UV Light is an effective treatment for many diseases : It is also found very effective in killing infectious bacteria, including AFB which causes tuberculosis.

In 1903 Dr. Niels Finsen of Denmark was awarded the Nobel Prize for being the first person to successfully treat skin tuberculosis with Ultra Violet Light.

It is very important to know and study in depth the UV Light and Infra Red Rays, but we must also know that too much UV light is bad, " we need a basic amount to support life and maintain a healthy immune system."

RHYTHM OF LIFE FROM SUNRISE TO SUNSET

From Sunrise to Sunset, the environment and color changes correspondingly affect all living things. The very first sunrise to the sunset of the present, we continue to be blessed by the beauty, power, life creating and life sustaining properties emanating from light. This is one of the important principles of Vastu Shastra.

Yoga & Meditation

- Increases energy and strength in the body
- Increases tolerance to stress
- Balances the breathing rhythm
- Increases storage of oxygen
- Increases ability of blood to absorb and carry oxygen.

The Cosmic Cycle :

The Cosmic Cycles affect our universe, which then affects the Solar System, which further affects the Earth's

Climate, season's inhabitants, right down to the smallest particle within an atom and exploring our external and internal environments. This is what Vastu Shastra explains.

WHAT THE VEDAS SAY :

Most of the present generation spends its working hours indoors eliminating the morning sunlight and fresh air from their daily needs.

So, it is very important to discuss and discover the indoor environment particularly in 21st Century, where the environment through out the world is becoming more and more polluted, in relation to our health, productivity and in general universal peace and well being.

Sanskrit Shloka: -

Shastrenanena Sarvasaya Lokasya Param Sukham I
Chaturvarga Phalaprapti Shlokashch Bhavedyuvam II
Shilpshastra Parigyan Mrityoapi Sujetam Vrajet I
Parmanand Janak Devanamidamiritam II
Shilp Vina Nahi Jagtishu Lokeshu Vidyate I Jagad Vina
Na Shilpanch Vertate Vasav Prabho II

Meaning : Because of Vastu Shastra the whole Universe gets good health, happiness and all-round prosperity. Human beings attain divinity with this knowledge. Followers of Vastu Shastra not only get worldly pleasures but also experience heavenly bliss.

"In this regard, Vedic Culture and Vastu Shastra play a very important role to help in building a clean environment, free from pollution of any kind, full of light and color needed for the development of a healthy NATION with a peaceful environment by balancing Man, Material and Nature within the framework of the Five Elements of Nature.

Here I would like to give a few important tips, especially to the Medical Practitioners to be adopted in

Hospitals and Nursing Homes for the speedy recovery of their patients.

The Vastu Research Centre, applying the following Vastu Principles to different patients, conducted a study.

The results revealed that 70% to 85% patients showed remarkable progress and their recovery rate was from 30% to 45% faster than the other patients.

1. *Orientation of Patient Room :*

- The Patient room should have plenty of, natural daylight with cross-ventilation, soft décor, fresh flowers, green plants and pleasant paintings or photographs on the walls.
- Have maximum openings (windows) on the N/E, East or S/E walls.
- No mirrors should be kept in the room
- Use only wooden beds and avoid steel or metal frame beds.

2. *Colour of the ceiling and three walls must be off-white and light green color on the west wall. Do not use any synthetic paints.*

3. *Electric wiring should be in conduit pipes with both ends properly earthed. Do not use fluorescent tube lights. Use only bulbs.*

4. *Use Window A/Cs only with Fresh Air vents in the "open" position. If using a central air conditioning with duct system, add minimum 15% to 20% fresh air.*

5. *No TV. Only pleasant soothing music or Bhajans for fixed times. Play soft instrumental music or some healing mantras and prayer for different patients in consultation with the Vastu Consultant.*

It was proved with evidence that patients who were given "distance prayer healing" recovered at a rate, which was 18% plus faster than other patients.

6. *Sleeping position:*

- Generally, in normal conditions, the patient's head should be towards the East.

- If there is excessive bleeding after the operation keep the head towards the North but only for a few days.
- For patients suffering from Asthma or breathing problems, the head should be towards the North-West.
- For patients suffering from Low Blood Pressure, Anaemia or Heart problems, their heads should be towards the South.
- Never keep the bed below a hanging beam.
- Pregnant ladies' heads should be towards the west. Never keep the head towards the North or South.
- After delivery keep the head towards the East.
- During the delivery, the overhead light in the OT Room should be switched off. Use normal indirect light.
- Never bring the newborn baby into bright light.
- Keep the baby in a room with pink walls, good eastern light and cross ventilation.

Towards the 21st Century Fogging the Atmosphere

Unless the preventive measures are taken by the year 2008, moving living and even breathing will be a problem in big cities with Generator sets and vehicular pollution accounting for 75 % of the air, noise and smoke pollution. Fogging the atmosphere further are the thermal power plants which contribute13% and assorted industrial activity that adds another 12%.

With the number of vehicles being added daily on the roads, the number of people injured or killed in road accidents has shot up by about 45% from 1990 by 2002.

Plastic and Solid Waste Management plans are just not in place. The present consumption patterns indicate that garbage volumes will more than double by the year 2005. This will leave 40 % of the total garbage scattered all over with no viable collection or recycling plan.

It is estimated that the total average energy consumed by man in the past 2000 years has been consumed in the last half century only.

Speed of human movement : The fastest transportation available to man for long distance travel was up to twenty miles per hour.

Today, men in space capsules are circling the earth at 30, 000Kmph.approx.

Development : The overwhelming majority of advanced technology and electronic equipments like TV, Computer, Telephone, Microwave Oven, etc, which we use in our daily life today, have been developed within the present lifetime.

What is evident from all the above examples is the fact that we are developing at an accelerated rate which itself is accelerating and leaving our own rich culture far behind.

However, the acceleration of change is going to deeply penetrate our private lives and will place absolutely unprecedented strains on the family. By 2015, an average adult may have to face eight times more stress.

Family of the future?

Career and status consciousness in the fair sex made life more mechanical and the time one spent with his family decreased still further. Now the possibilities are threefold:

1. Family life will be dead except for the first few years of child raising.
2. The family is for a Golden Age:

With advances in Information Technology, homes and offices will become coincident. People may not have to move out of their homes because they would be able to do most of their jobs and shopping from their homes on E-mail, Web Site or on the Internet. As free time and leisure increases, the families will spend more time together and will derive great satisfaction from joint activity.

The future is more open than it might appear. The family may either vanish or entering a new Golden Age, it may break up and shatter only to come together again in weird and novel ways like contract marriages.

Let us discuss some possibilities, which may revolutionize the concept of family altogether as compared to the Vedic Age.

Concept Of Motherhood ?

The birth technology is going to have the most upsetting effect on family.

The extension of the test tube baby concept may lead to babies which can be grown in a laboratory jar. What happens to the notion of maternity then? And what happens to the self- image of the female in societies.

Birth of the Super Human?

Skin grafting techniques are commonly employed these days in plastic surgery and allied fields. In fact, if the top R & D people of surgery are to be believed, very shortly human limbs can be developed in labs. It might be possible within next 25 to 50 years to develop the human brain in laboratories. Brain transplants can come even sooner.

Lord Shiva had transplanted an elephant head to the human body.

Ancient Egyptians used to keep their dead bodies inside a pyramid properly preserved in the hope that some day it might be possible to inject life back into them.

Medical Researchers are actively involved in research in which probably they think, it will be possible to do so now.

All of these are likely to cause great social stresses. In fact, the final question arises if life and death can also be governed by human beings what happens to our concept of God? And who, in that case, will control all these the super - humans with super brains or the technocrats?

Finally, who is going to decide which individual is to be converted into a super-human?

Will the concept of "crime & punishment" change?

Will the concept of "power & ego" hazards vanish?

Will life become so mechanical that everyone does a set of jobs, which have been pre-programmed in his mind?

If life becomes so mechanical then what right will we have to call ourselves human being? Will we not be reduced to being machines?

All these possibilities need to be given further thought so that we are prepared to face them whenever they crop up.

The answer lies with the Vedas and in the Vedic knowledge.

10

True Happiness

To be happy for no reason is the happiness. Happiness for a reason is just another form of misery, because the reason can be questioned at any stage or time.

Generally we say we are happy because we have good friends, because I have nice family, because I have a great job, because I have money, because I have a nice beautiful home, because I am healthy without any disease, because I have security in my life etc. All these reasons for happiness are tenuous because they come and go like the passing breeze. But when happiness eludes, we seek pleasure through addictive behaviours in the unconscious hope that we will find joy. External causes never create real joy. Joy is an internal state of consciousness that determines how we perceive the world.

The internal source of joy is our connection to our creator, our source, our inner self is the cause, while happiness is its effect.

Why do we seek happiness from outside of ourselves ?

We come into the world as a result of others actions. We survive in dependence on others. We humans are social beings.

Whether we like it or not, there is hardly a moment in

our lives when we do not benefit from others' activities. For this reason it is hardly surprising that most of our happiness arises in the context of our relationships with others.

So we learn from a young age to rely on others rather than on ourselves. If we rely on others for our food, shelter and other needs, why not happiness ? Well happiness of course does come from many things and our social relationships and other external factors can bring us much joy, but many of us have not connected with ourselves as we have connected with others. The negative side is that placing all of your happiness in the hands of others will lead to a lot of pain and disappointment throughout your life.

True happiness cannot be sought outside of yourself not in your relationship with others, the groups you belong to, or in the things around you. Unless you can stand alone in your own shadow and feel happiness from within, true happiness may always elude you for external things come and go like the tide.

The only constant aspect in your life is you. Love you, admire you, value you and be happy to be you.

No matter how much you love a partner, a child, or a friend, you cannot make your happiness conditional upon them. Why? Because you will have certain expectations of others and when those expectations are not met, you may feel hurt, betrayed, misunderstood, taken for granted, invalidated, confused and so on.

Everyone is an individual. We have each grown to develop our own sets of values, beliefs, attitudes and ways of looking at the world. Our views may not be exactly the same as our loved ones. However, we often expect those loved ones to know what we want from them.

HAPPINESS IS WITHIN EXPANSION OF SELF THE INFINITE IN THE FINITE.

If you have lost touch with your internal source of joy, if the happiness you experience always originates with circumstances outside yourself, then you are at the mercy of every situation and every stranger you meet. This kind of happiness is ever illusive.

If you keep your face to the sunshine, you cannot see your shadows. Just as a beautiful sunrise might be hidden by the clouds, so too, our inner happiness is also hidden behind our everyday concerns. Social conditioning and constricted awareness keep us from glimpsing this kingdom of heaven hidden in the depths of our heart. But we can learn to rise above the clouds of conditioning and rediscover the source of joy deep within us.

The greatest discovery of mankind is that we can change, alter or mould our life, or create an envornment around us by altering our attitude through our trained mind.

In today's world, there is a lot of stress. Youngsters today are very competitive and the world is equally challenging. In such a situation, it is very important to be calm. I believe meditation or going for spirituality classes is a welcome trend. However, one should ensure that it does not become an addiction.

Wearing lucky charms is something I just don't believe in. I would advise youngsters to not believe in superstition and rather be nice to everyone. Once you do that, the world will be nice to you. Believe in karma and you will get everything. You will reach God if you do good to others. I teach the same to my students.

Hard work always helps, but it is equally important to be passionate about whatever you do. If you remember God in every breath you take, your tensions will vanish and sooner or later you will emerge successful.

If you analyse yourself, why you are disappointed or

hurt. You may find your initial thoughts or statements begin with "Because he did" or "Because she did not". Now look deeper to the true reason for your disappointment. Such statements will start with "Because I expected", "because I wanted" or "Because I thought he or she should"

You truly only ever have control over yourself and realising this can save you a lot of pain. Of course you can be disappointed in others but you have no control over their actions and reactions. You can share the reasons for your disappointment but you cannot expect the other person or situation to change because the other person has as free will.

When you realise that you are responsible for your thinking and expectations, you will start to see that you have placed much of your happiness in the hands of others. You can now take your power back by recognizing that you have the choice to react to something either negatively or positively. By making your happiness conditional upon another person, you hand your power over to them. You feel a 'victim' whenever things do not go as you want or expect. In doing this, you set yourself up pain. But you can now turn this around and instead set yourself up for happiness.

The key is to not expect a particular outcome. What happens next is up to you. You can choose to wallow in negative feelings which may further damage a relationship, or you can try to place a positive spin on the situation. Perhaps you can find your happiness in the fact that you have done your part in dealing with the situation by getting your issue out into the open. Realise that it may not be an issue to the other person, but ideally you will work together to reach a compromise. You can also decide to be happy for the other person and the pain they show you because it helps you to grow. There are always choices and different ways of looking at the same thing.

It puts things into perspective when you resign yourself to the fact that people do make mistakes they forget things, they do not think properly, they do not always consider how others may be affected by their actions, they can act selfishly at times, and so on. We are all humans and we are designed to make mistakes as they are our greatest opportunities to learn. "All seasons are beautiful for the person who carries happiness within."

I would never guide you to ask for predictions and outcomes as this is entirely disempowering. Moreover, you will not receive them from God because life is meant to be lived and experienced in the moment. It is in the moment that you need the guidance. Naturally, one moment will lead to the next.

Please always remember that whenever you are not sure about what to do in any situation, or concerning any event, such as what to do when so and so comes over to your house a few days from now, you can always ask for advance information to guide you concerning that situation. This is not asking about an outcome. This is asking for guidance about a situation facing you, and one that you may either be upset over or unsure about now. If you are not sure about something, ask God!.

To believe or not to believe is the basic issue. If one is to believe, one should believe in whom? In God? Or in those who deny the existence of God? Or in those who believe in God? Or in that person who claims he himself is the God? Ignorance is not the ensure.

All realized souls say:- live in the plenitude of the present, the past is dead and gone, the future is yet to come and dark, only the present is true, therefore it is important to live **LIFE BEFORE DEATH.**

Faith is absolutely essential for anything to happen. Without faith, even the master- disciple relationship does not blossom.

The most fortunate happening of our existence is that

we are born as "HUMAN BEING" with super faculties. It is therefore impotent to express gratitude to God for his mercies, but also to ensure that the human body so gifted by the nature, is properly maintained.

We spend one third of our life by sleeping and rest of our life earning, out of that half our lives ruining our health by not careing or living against nature, and the other half taking care of it.

Sanskrit Shlokas

> dhyayato visayan pumsah
> sangas tesupajayate
> sagat sanjayate kamah
> kamat krodho' bhijayate

Bhagavad-Gita 2(62)

> **Meaning :** While contemplating the objects of the senses, a person develops attachment for them, and from such attachment lust develops, and from lust anger arises.

One who is not Kirshna conscious is subjected to material desires while contemplating the objects of senses. The senses require real engagements, and if they are not engaged in the transcendental loving service of the Lord, they will certainly seek engagement in the service of materialism. In the material world everyone, including Lord Siva and Lord Brahma-to say nothing of other demigods in the heavenly planets-is subjected to the influence of sense objects, and the only method to get out of this puzzle of material existence is to become Krishna conscious.

Lord Siva was deep in meditation, but when Parvati agitated him for sense pleasure, he agreed to the proposal, and as a result Kartikeya was born. When Haridasa Thakur was a young devotee of the Lord, he was similarly allured by the incarnation of Maya Devi, but Haridasa easily passed the test because of his unalloyed devotion to Lord Krishna.

As illustrated in the above-mentioned verse of Sri Yamunacarya, a sincere devotee of the Lord shuns all material sense enjoyment due to his higher taste for spiritual enjoyment in the association of the Lord.

That is the secret of success. One who is not, therefore, in Krishna consciousness, however powerful he may be in controlling the senses by artificial repression, is sure ultimately to fail, for the slightest thought of sense pleasure will agitate him to gratify his desires.

Sanskrit Shlokas

Krodhad bhavati sammohah
sammohat smrti-vibhramah
smrti-bhramsad buddhi-naso
buddhi-nasat pranasyati

Bhagavad-Gita 2(63)

Meaning : From anger, delusion arises, and from delusion bewilderment of memory. When memory is bewildered, intelligence is lost, and when intelligence is lost, one falls down again into the material pool.

By development of Krishna consciousness one can know that everything has its use in the service of the Lord. Those who are without knowledge of Krsna consciousness artificially try to avoid material objects, and as a result, although they desire liberation from material bondage, they do not attain to the perfect stage of renunciation.

On the other hand, a person in Krishna consciousness knows how to use everything in the service of the Lord; therefore he does not become a victim of material consciousness. For example, for an impersonalist, the Lord, or the Absolute, being impersonal, cannot eat. Whereas an imperonalist tries to avoid good eatables, a devotee knows that Krishna is the supreme enjoyer and that He eats all that is offered to Him in devotion.

So, after offering good eatables to the Lord, the devotee takes the remnants, called prasadam. Thus everything becomes spiritualized and there is no danger of a downfall. The devotee takes prasadam in Krishna consciousness, whereas the nondevotee rejects it as material.

The impersonalist, therefore, cannot enjoy life due to his artificial renunciation; and for this reason, a slight agitation of the mind pulls him down again into the pool of material existence. It is said that such a soul, even though rising up to the point of liberation, falls down again due to his not having support in devotional service.

Sanskrit Shloka

sreyan sva-dharmo vigunah
para-dharmat svanusthitat
sva-dharme nidhanam sreyah
para-dharmo bhayavahah

Bhagavad-Gita 3(35)

Meaning : It is far better to discharge one's prescribed duties, even though they may be faulty, than another's duties. Destruction in the course of performing one's own duty is better than engaging in another's duties, for to follow another's path is dangerous.

One should therefore discharge his prescribed duties in full Krishna consciousness rather than those prescribed for others. Prescribed duties complement one's psychophysical condition, under the spell of the modes of material nature. Spiritual duties are as ordered by the spiritual master, for the transcendental service of Krishna. But both materially or spiritually, one should stick to his prescribed duties even up to death, rather than imitate another's prescribed duties.

Duties on the spiritual platform and duties on the material platform may be different, but the principle of following the authorized direction is always good for the performer. When one is under the spell of the modes of material nature, one should follow the prescribed rules for particular situations and should not imitate others. For example, a brahmana, who is in the mode of goodness, is nonviolent, whereas a *khsatriya,* who is in the mode of passion, is allowed to be violent. As such, for a *khsatriya* it is better to be vanquished following the rules of violence than to imitate a brahmana who follows the principles of nonviolence.

Everyone has to cleanse his heart by a gradual process, not abruptly. However, when one transcends the modes of material nature and is fully situated in Krishna consciousness, he can perform anything and everything under the direction of the bona fide spiritual master. In that complete stage of Krishna consciousness, the *Khsatriya* may act as a *brahmana,* or a *brahmana* may act as a *khsatriya.* In the transcendental stage, the distinctions of the material world do not apply. For example, Visvamitra was originally a *khsatriya,* but later on he acted as a *brahmana,* whereas Parasurama was a *brahmana,* but later on he acted as a *ksatriya.* Being transcendentally situated, they could do so; but as long as one is on the material platform, he must perform his duties according to the modes of material nature. At the same time, he must have a full sense of Krishna consciousness.

11

One Life to Live and One Life to Love

The nature has gifted us the beautiful world, and the perfect body to enjoy the gift of nature. It is believed that after millions of re-birth we get this human body. The nature has gifted us five senses and the brain to control our five senses to improve the quality of life.

I believe we have one present life to live. We must make best use of creativity and live a useful life not only for our self but for our society and country.

Happiness is not the ultimate destination. In fact, the successful journey itself can bring fulfillment and happiness but not without the spiritual aspect. Mind, body and soul are interlinked and inseparable. We must know the art of balancing man, and material with Nature.

In the course of living life truthfully, one can be overwhelmed by the compelling, dazzling aura that surrounds entrepreneurial success. Then one wonders about the values of life.

What is values of life?

(a) Name
(b) Fame
(f) Education
(g) Leadership

(c) Money
(d) Properties
(e) Wealth
(h) Spirituality
(i) Healthy life
(j) Wellbeing
(k)Good family background

After possessing every materialistic thing as mentioned above are we happy? Are we satisfied? Are we spreading love? Or are we getting a proper respect or love from others?, if we put this question to our self, the answer we get will be "**not yet satisfied**".

When we touch any elder's or saint's feet they bless us with Deerghashman Bhava's (long life, health and happiness). Those blessings become true only when the society is filled with good health and development.

But in reality the people in the society are not living their healthy life. As the statistical surveys shows that "Billions of people are suffering from "Diabetes, TB, Cancer, Stress, B.P." etc.

Apart from the availability of advanced medical facilities, corporate hospitals, thousands of doctors and medicines, people are still suffering from many diseases and also with the reactions caused by the medicines.

In Vedas it is stated that Nature cure is a great doctor. As to keep all his creations (living beings) he created nature as the health centre, plants and trees as powerful medicines. As all the power of nature is being destroyed by the social animals (human beings) all the diseases are born.

In Vedas it is mentioned that if we perform auspicious functions like poojas, yagnas, traditional customs and helping others we can get remedies for all the diseases and /problems. The best remedies are also given in branches of Vedas like Ayurveda and other subjects.

But the present generation has forgotten all these things and started adopting different diseases. To get into practice all the forgotten Vedas, Spirituals, and Vedic medicines we have to live with the nature.

When we talk about Vedas, we are talking about knowledge. Vedas means knowledge. The mind possesses knowledge, therefore, the mind is the main author of all our actions and behavior.

Human beings take birth on this planet based on the composition of the five elements of nature. We take birth with five senses, but it is essential to develop these five senses through knowledge. Knowledge comes from the Vedas and development comes from the mind.

We may possess the best knowledge, but the use of this knowledge is not through Karmas (action). It is our mind which assimilates this knowledge and puts it to the proper use.

In other words, the mind is the author, the principal, the thinker, the planner, the subject as well as the object, behind all our actions. If so, why not discuss about the mind, with the mind, for the mind. The mind that is ageless and requires no rest.

Sanskrit Shlokas: -

> " Na pranena na apranena martyo jivati Kaschana ,
> Itarcna tu jivanti yasmin etavapasritau."
>
> **Meaning :** Our life system is not dependant merely on the process of breathing. The intake of diet is indeed important for health, but health does not rest on food alone. The entire system can be thrown out of gear if the mind is upset. A mild turbulence injected into the mind is enough to disturb the entire balance of personality.

YOUR STRENGTH IS IN YOU. RELIGION BEGINS WHERE SCIENCE ENDS; THE BEGINNING OF THE HIGHER WISDOM.

This compilation is an humble attempt to discover the synchronization of Vedic Knowledge with Vastu Shastra. Present day life in the 21st Century has become complicated, illogical and contradictory. Any attempt to describe this period fully would run into volumes, yet the end would still be nowhere in sight!

As explained earlier, I have attempted to take a microscopic section from the magnificent Vedic period based on 'Truth' and scientific reason to show how close people are to nature and how they could learn the art of meaningful and fruitful living aided by Vedic knowledge to enjoy the gift of nature.

Vedas regulate the relation between man and his environments. A learner should exhibit his skill by overcoming the difficulties and differences between the principles laid down in the 'Vedas' and the need of the present day requirements, keeping in mind the original relation between man and nature and to find acceptable solutions.

For good results it is all the more important to put the correct question rather than to find the correct answers to the wrong questions.

We have to create harmony between the common values, moral codes, individual beliefs, ideological convictions, economic conditions, social obligations and cultural symbolizations coupled with philosophical ideas and meaningful environment. During the Vedic period, people built homes, temples and hermitages not merely to be used as shelter but mainly with a view to have a peaceful place for offering prayers, find peace and to live in common harmony. The ancient philosophic concept represents two different logical processes the 'Inductive' and 'Deductive'.

The former took its stand upon 'Smriti' or reasoned knowledge and law of cause and effect and the latter dependent upon insight or inspiration, known as 'Shruti' or divine revelation of which the Vedas are said to be the expression.

In modern language we may call these as an objective or atheistic and subjective or theistic science towards the finer and subtler aspects of life and consciousness.

The Vedas propound that apart from the physical body; an individual constitutes his mind and his intellect and is presided over or enlivened by the Cosmic Consciousness.The mind function is two fold, to acquire knowledge through the five senses (Gyan Indrias) and to act in the world outside through the five related organs (Karam Indrias).

The five basic elements of nature, namely, the space, air, fire, water and earth correspond to the sensations of hearing, touch, sight, taste and smell, respectively. Intellect is the discriminating power in us, to take a decision for elevation to righteousness or to indulge in sensual short lived pleasures; to endeavor to rediscover alpha and omega of the reality or to succumb to desires and remain in worldly illusions.

An open secret, relatively unknown, is that India is a source, the fountainhead of the vast ancient Vedic knowledge available on this planet today. When the Vedic concept is presented through modern technological advances, the sublime information becomes available to all walks of life and can be easily understood. This would give a new outlook to the world of modern living with high thinking.

12

Learn to Love and Love Yourself

Human beings are more spiritual beings than physical or material beings. External gratification cannot give them the ultimate peace of mind. Happiness comes from within. This world is an illusion and it is changing everyday. One should learn to live in the present. Enjoy this moment to the fullest.

I enjoy achieving material benefits - be it money, awards or recognition. However, if I am doing something, I have to plunge into it completely and enjoy it. If I do not enjoy, any external achievement it will be just a shame. The root cause of sorrow is expectation. You are always asking for something from this world and when you do not get it, you are disappointed. So, do not expect anything and keep doing what you enjoy and you will get your much deserved happiness.

A man will become an expert when he stop thinking. One is not necessarily born with courage, but one is born with potential. Without courage, we cannot practice any other virtue with consistency. We cannot be kind, true, merciful or generous.

However brilliant an action may be, it should not be accounted as great when it is not the result of a great purpose.

Ability is what you are capable of doing. Motivation determines what you do. Attitude determines how well you do it.

How much you are the person you want to be is determined by the way you act and react and the choices you make. When you take a risk and start to get to know yourself, you confront the way you carry love into the world. This confronts your faith your trust your ability to let love into your life.

Learning to love involves learning to face yourself, and accepting responsibility to become the person you want to be. God is always there with you like your inner dialogue, whether you are listening or not.

Being able to accept love comes when you are ready to hear loving messages from yourself and others. Are you ready ? Are you listening ?

I believe in love at first sight. Because I loved my mother ever since I opened my eyes.

Learning to love yourself is essential in the development of the ability to act in loving ways with others. If you always focus on your own faults you will most likely highlight the shortcomings of others.

The critical self-talk will spill into your conversations and you will be known as a negative person, a faultfinder. If you do tend to center on the mistakes of others, consider what was programmed into your thinking when you were growing up. How did your parents speak to you ? How do you speak to your children ? Are you creating fault finders?

While much of the responsibility of parenting is teaching, it need not be constant criticism. Good parenting involves accepting mistakes and teaching correct ways to live with patience and love. Were you allowed to make mistakes and learn from them when you were growing up or were there constant expectations of perfection ? Were you belittled and made to feel as if you were not lovable ?

Now change some of the negative works to positive words. Could you say these statements about yourself in public ? Would you classify this as selfish and bragging! Is it more acceptable to you to be derogatory and denounce your God given gifts and charming qualities ? Is criticism more familiar to you than praise ?

Rigid thinking and fear: Often the critical persons are fearful of being or doing the very thing they criticise others about, so they make a great attempt to appear perfect. Putting others down so they feel one up, is a natural way they feed and hide their sense of not really being as good as others.

Behaving in this superior way is the opposite to living a life from a focus of love.

Love involves opening up of our selves, heart, mind and soul. It means we risk letting others see who we really are and trusting that we are in fact lovable. Looking at your self in the mirror can be a scary adventure. Seeing who is looking back, straight in the eye, confronts you with your perception of the person you have become. Do you have the courage to be honest with yourself ?

Our mothers, fathers, family and society all supported this idea that you should go through the formative years of your life, and perhaps all of your life, living within a basic belief system that says you are separate from all people and things in this life, including God. Hey, that is okay. That is what is so. But now you are waking up. Now you absolutely know that you are free to choose all things in life, even something as powerful as your overall belief system.

Now you are aware of the fact that there is another belief system in existence that you are free to choose to live by, if you so desire. What would make you desire to take on this life changing experience of living within a love based belief system of oneness ? You have been told most of your life to take the easy way, even if it turns out to be harder in the end. You know in your heart that the decision to change your belief system will require effort on your part. Is it worth if ? The rewards of taking on this challenge must be worth the effort because there are no guarantees. Or are there?

This is **Life Before Death**, I am talking about here. The process of life does not come with guarantees when you live within the fear-based belief of separation. You can live the most virtuous life imaginable but you will still not be guaranteed a spot in heaven.

The only guarantee that fear-based thinking gives you is that you have the opportunity to gain entrance into heaven. You are not guaranteed entrance but you are guaranteed the opportunity. Pretty weak isn't it ? The love based paradigm of oneness holds out some very tempting rewards.

First of all, you are guaranteed an everlasting life. You are eternal, just like God. You are guaranteed the ability to create your life according to your intentions and desires. You are doing that right now but you may not be conscious of that fact.

You are guaranteed heaven because, whether you know it or not, you are in heaven right now. You just can not recognize it because you are unconscious of this fact, and you probably believe heaven to be in some other form than this paradise we call earth. Let's put it this way. You are in heaven if you choose that to be so.

Confidence: Never come with having all the answers, it comes from being open to the questions.

A strong positive mental attitude will create more miracles than any wonder drug.

Love is living in the world today, and manifests in the actions of human beings. Can you see love looking back ? Is the God in whom you believe a God of criticism and struggle or of acceptance and love ? There is also great evil, distrust and hate in the world today.

Violence in our society in our homes and family relationships reveal it. We must cast the evil out of our lives and confront with trust and courage the values that are core of a loving life.

Love is not placid and passive. Love is passionate and active. Each small step an individual takes, to replace lies with truth, criticism with praise, fear with love, is a step to a new way of living. Live in trust that God's support is present in your life. This is what doing the work of a loving supreme force is all about. Work with the loving force!

Tears can be more special than smiles.

Smiles can be given to anyone, but tears are shed for people we love.

If you met a person who has lost his / her smile, kindly give your, which is free of cost.

Slow down and enjoy life. It's not only the scenery you miss by going too fast but you also miss the sense of where you are going and why.

Love is not one way, or for one person to other person, or a reflector, more love is give or take. You can explore your love with so many ways and feel the satisfaction.

You can love to God. You love your parents, your sisters, brothers, relatives and family. You can love your neighbor, society and your country. You make your colleges/ classmate your friends because you love them.

You love the nature, you love waterfalls, green trees, flowers, flow of water, different seasons, change of weather, and so on. You love music, art, colour etc.

This love is permanent without any expectations. Therefore you enjoy this and love them, in return they gives you peace and relaxation.

Some loves are temporary, because they are exiting, demanding, expect return, this type of love are full of eggs, and satisfy the body need, this love is diluted with the sex action.

This type of love is full of excitement and lust, it is alive till you are attracted to the object or the beauty.

You do love heart to heart, your love is limited and a particular attraction, make you attracted to somebody's beauty, or body, or his or her style, or you are attracted to their voice, their style, way of make up, clothing, his or her, I. Q, smartness etc.

But this type of qualities are temporary and not permanent.

I believe in destiny. I think everything is pre-written and nothing can be rewritten. Just because you worship God regularly, it does not mean you can change your destiny. Whatever is destined will happen, but what you can do is keep trying. And, praying to God will give you the strength to face the difficulties that life has to offer.

13

Learn to Listen Your Own Intuition

As you go through the decisions that you make in your daily life, how much do you rely on your intuition?

Have you been true to yourself ? Have you been following your own intuition, or conscious to you heart, believing in yourself, trusting your very own belief ?

Do you feel focused and strong in the choices that you make ?

Or do you feel that you have to deliberate, analyse, weigh out pros and cons, get lots of opinions from friends or family and scare your-self into a decision ? Maybe you are one to make a quick decision and then second guess it to the point that you undo what you believed in ?

Or has this thought never even occurred to you before?

Now that you are reading this chapter in Life Before Death, give yourself this chance and ask yourself this question. Be true and answer it honestly. It is a very simple question to answer is not it ? To answer it, say either 'yes' or 'no'. It is as simple as that! But very often, things are not that simple for many. You might be one of them.

Living as we do in a modernised, fast-changing, ever-developing time, it is indeed hard for things to be that simple. Everyone of us is, in a way, forced to keep up with the pace, brainwashed to just believe in the system. We are taught to believe that in order to survive and to be successful, we have to follow what is laid down for us, follow what everyone else is doing; that we should be doing this and not doing that.

But are you not the one who is supposed to be telling yourself what you should do, rather than being told by others? The sad truth is, many of us unknowingly live our lives, only to be consumed by regret in our later years; when it is too late to do anything. It is a scary thought, isn't it ?

Now, this is certainly not the way life should be. To begin with, life should not be this stressful. Yes, to constantly learn and to improve ourselves is what we should be doing. But you should not lose your direction, drifting further and further away from the real one.

Are you on the real direction you now? You have to understand this. Right within you there exists two states, your inner self and your outer self. Your inner self is made up of your thoughts and beliefs, your outer self comprises of the actions which support your inner thoughts. To put it simply, your inner self plus your outer self equal to the real you.

To be the real you, your inner self and outer self must complement one another: Remember this. You came into this world with a journey of your own to discover. This life journey is yours and yours alone and nobody else's. You decide for yourself what you want. It is not for others to decide for you. If you have to please someone, please yourself, not somebody else.

The mind itself must also become a subject of enquiry. When both the world and the mind are closely studied and examined, the seeker cannot escape concluding that each is dependent upon the other. Neither the mind nor the world can exist independent of each other. Dependence is a clear clue to conclude that the phenomena are unreal.

The sooner one understands the whole inner process aimed at increasing the purity and refinement of the inner mind and the still inner intellect, the better for him. Only when he focuses all his efforts in this direction, he stands the chance of discovering the ultimate truth, the reality of the indwelling Self.

For all that exists in this world, there is always the equal and the opposite side. But though they may be opposing, they are at all times interrelating. This is the natural way of life. When there is day there will be night. When there is a positive there will be a negative. When there are strengths, there will also be weaknesses. The list goes on.

Similarly within you, when you can be happy you can be unhappy too. Surely, happiness is what you seek in life? So, be true to yourself! It is only when you are true to yourself that you will find happiness. Instead of listening to others to allow them to tell you that you shouldn't do this and that, you tell yourself that you must do this and you must do that! Instead of listening to others, listen to your own intuition.

We all have had our rounds of confusion and analysis paralysis. The one conclusion is that logic alone does not work. And the answer is to learn how to use a tool that you were actually born with. That tool is your intuition. We hear the words 'surrender', 'trust' and 'let go' all the time. But what does that really mean? And what are we surrendering to? Our logic tells us this is dangerous. So our best attempts to let go last a few minutes and then we are back to trying to figure it all out!

What is right and what is wrong? There is never a definite right or wrong. You do what you think is right for yourself. Just picture this scenario. Right from the time that we are children, we have been taught over and over again that it is a sin to lie. Now, let me ask you something. If you can actually save a person's life by telling a kind lie, would you? Suppose telling a kind lie would result in him being spared and given another chance, while telling the truth would mean that the poor man would lose his life. Now, which is a sin, to tell a lie or to indirectly murder someone? The line between being a saint or a murderer is a thin one.

Similarly, there is a thin line between a happy and unhappy person. Which side of the line do you want to be? To be a truthfully happy person, your actions must complements your thoughts and belief. You have to understand this. Even the slightest decision can affect your life. Sometimes having just a few additional minutes of sleep can make a difference to your day. Those few minutes could decide whether you will have an efficient day or a bad one.

Seek the correct way of life. Be true to yourself and you are bound to find happiness.

Your intuition is comprised of the energetic senses that you were born with to assist you in staying connected to your higher or inner self.

We are always connected to that power greater than our physical selves and that connection is our intuition. I have taught classes on Letting Go and while people have the best of intentions think that what really holds them back is a lack of trust.

That is because we do not understand the mystery of our intuition.

So here are key points for you to consider that will hopefully help you get a better handle on the most powerful sense that you have.

1. Everyone is born with intuition and has the ability to

develop it to be strong and reliable.

2. Intuition is always the most efficient and accurate advice that you can get about any issue, concern or desire.

3. Our society encourages us to ignore our intuition and focus strictly on logic. We disengage from our energetic senses and end up feeling very confused, anxious and taking a very long slow road to happiness. Your intuition is always working whether you focus on it or not! When you harness the power of your intuition you are able to fully access your personal power. Not using your intuition is like having eyes and ears and ignoring or fighting their functions. Your eyes and ears are on your head and whether you are concentrating on using them or not they are always working.

   They become very powerful tools when you deliberately focus your sight or hearing! Think of how hard it would be to watch a wonderful movie or listen to a beautiful symphony without your ears or eyes! Unwavering trust begins with knowing your intuition and how to use it!

4. Your intuition is your direct and absolute link to communication with spirit.

5. Your intuitive senses lay over your physical senses. We get energetic or intuitive feelings through energetic sight, energetic hearing (you hear a small voice that gives you a warning or feels like a hunch to follow), energetic feeling (a gut feeling in your stomach that feels like butterflies or goose bumps) and energetic knowing (feeling like you just know how to do something or how a situation will turn out without learning or cause).

6. To create positive energies around you, I suggests, to balance these two energies within man plus material

with nature, with an objective to achieve wealth (Artha) for a comfortable life (Karma) and to lead a glorious life (Dharma).

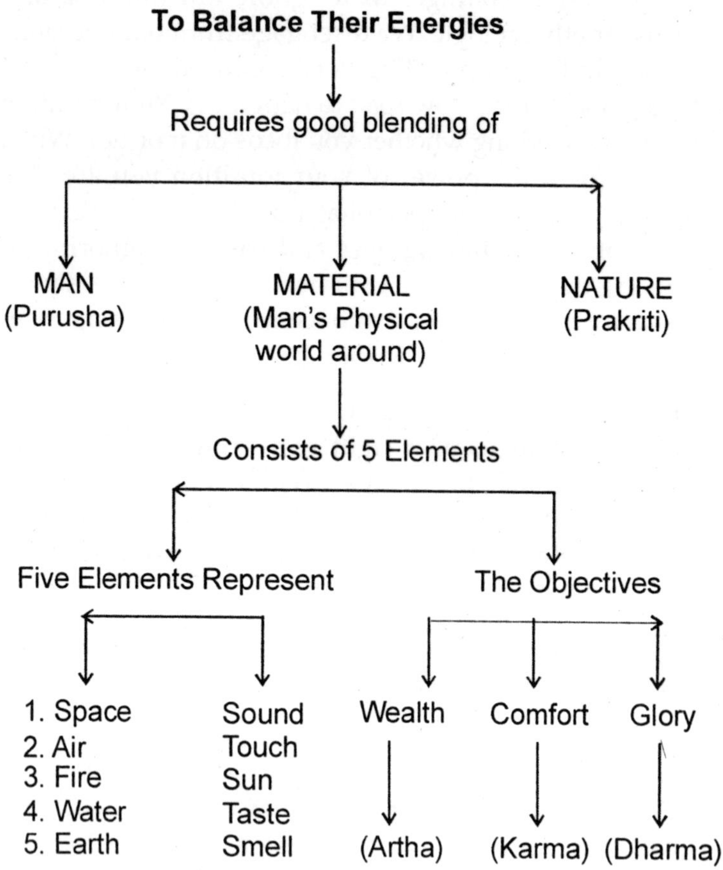

To keep the total balance of combination "Man, Material and Nature" in relation with five elements.

To balance the energies in relationship with human comfort level

From the **Space**

1. Basic Elements	Cosmos rays
2. Technological Field	Vibration
3. Instrument of Perception:	
a). To acquire inward	Ear
b). To acquire outward	Speech
4. Work Organs	Communication
5. Controlling Central Force:	Mind
a). Flow of Thoughts	
b). Emotions or joy	
6. The Presiding Force	Cosmos rays
7. Supreme Energy	Soul (prana)

Energy transformation related to man material and technology.

(a) Silence

(b) Acoustics

(c) Reflection

(d) Vibrations

(e) Texture surfaces

(f) Texture forms

(g) Design language system

(h) Non-measurable Dimensions Depicting Mental comforts.

From the **Air**

1. Basic Elements	Touch
2. Technological Field	Climate
3. Instrument of Perception:	
a). To acquire inward	Skin
b). To acquire outward	Finger
4. Work Organs	Hands
5. Controlling Central Force:	Weather Conditioning
6. The Presiding Force	Circulation Symtem

Energy transformation Related to man Material and Technology.

(a) Climatology: To study and Apply in Daily life

From the **Sun (Fire)**

1. Basic Elements	Sun
2. Technological Field	Light
3. Instrument of Perception:	
a). To acquire inward	Eyes
b). To acquire outward	Heat
4. Work Organs	Light and Heat
5. Controlling Central Force:	Color
6. The Presiding Force	Texture (Visual)

Energy Transformation Related to man Material and Technology.

(a) Light

(b) Color

(c) Solar System (Gain or Loss)

From **Water**

1. Basic Elements	Taste
2. Technological Field	Life Source
3. Instrument of Perception:	
a). To acquire inward	Toungue
b). To acquire outward	Sweating
4. Work Organs	ANUS (Lower Part of the Canal)
5. Controlling Central Force:	River
a). River	
b). well	
c). Tube well	
6. The Presiding Force	Sea

Energy Transformation Related to man Material and Technology.

a) Plumbing

b) Heating and Cooling

c) Water supply system Network and Disposal

d) Sewerage System

e) Drainage System

f) Flora, Waterfall, Fountain, Pool

g) Water Management

h) Water Engineering

From **Earth**

1. Basic Elements	Smell
2. Technological Field	Basic Raw Material
3. Instrument of Perception:	
a). To acquire inward	Nose
b). To acquire outward	Nose
4. Work Organs	Genitals Procreate
5. Controlling Central Force:	Formation
6. The Presiding Force	Mud (Earth)

Energy Transformation related to man Materials and Technology.

a) Basic Building Raw Materials
b) Mud Architecture are famous internationally
c) Landscape
d) Insulation
e) Recycling

So many people call me for readings and want me to confirm for them that their future outcomes of various hopes or problems will be exactly as I predict. This is so disempowering. Real trust comes from having a direct communication with yourself through understanding, recognising and knowing how to use and rely on your intuition!

I have done hundreds of intuitive readings for clients and the ones who really do the best after the reading is over are the ones who take responsibility for themselves and use their intuition in combination with their creative problem solving tools like logic to decide what to do next.

When we ignore our intuition we feel anxious, confused and uneasy. We may feel intellectually that it is the right decision but something still doesn't feel certain. So we decide to take lots and lots of action to leave no stone unturned.

When we use our intuition it may seem illogical but our decision feels right. It feels like a sense of knowing or certainty that you may not be able to describe. And your actions feel inspired. You feel led as opposed to running after an outcome. You feel guided to take inspired action and your hunch feels like a knowing instead of a reckless risk.

It's time to empower yourself by harnessing your own intuition! When you take the time to learn about, understand and tap into your intuition, you will find that your decisions and actions are so much easier to make!

You will live so much more powerfully and efficiently. Your tasks will be done in a fraction of the time because you will be working from certainty instead of fear! You may consider the opinions of other for a perspective but you will know that your intuition has the final say!

This is the real powerful **Life Before Death**.

14

Accept Life As It Is (The God Gifted You)

Accept life as it is, the God has gifted you. Fighting against life's realities and adopting a stance of negativism only creates unnecessary pain and difficulty in you life.

Accepting life as such allows you to understand your frustrations, grow from them and experience life's abundance.

Life, no matter how we choose to look at it, is a challenge. It is the beginning of a struggle that continues until we breathe our last breath. Life is something that we did not request. None of us asked to be born. Neither did we ask to be poor or wealthy, tall or short. We did not ask to be a part of one family as opposed to another.

Life is full of risks. There is a certain element of risk taking that is inherent in every venture we undertake; whether it is in business, or in marriage, in a profession or in athletics. We never have complete security within ourselves. For we know that every moment we live, our lives are in constant danger. A stray bullet may hit us, a car emerging out of nowhere may crush us, and a slip of the foot may result in our death. So life is unpredictable. We get no warning, we are afforded no red alert, and we get no second chance at life.

We might as well face the fact that our life is a dying life. As soon as we are born, we begin to die and every day we manage to somehow survive, we have only taken another step towards our grave. Each morning when we wake up from a refreshing sleep, we have died a little during the night.

Those living on the highest levels of life have learned to accept life on its own terms.

There are some realities about life that we must accept. This is the key to living joyfully in communion with the heavenly while abiding here on this earth planet. **He who wants a rose must respect the thorn**.

When one door closes, another opens for us, but some time we often look so long and so regretfully upon the closed door, that we do not see the one which has opened for us.

Understanding life helps you make the unconscious conscious; to see your misguided beliefs and negativity clearly, to understand their roots and causes, and most importantly to transform them. A complete path, it offers a practical, rational, honest, and above all, gentle and self-accepting way to move from an attitude of you versus the world to one of you and the world; from you versus life.

Fundamental to accepting life is to give recognition to the supreme life-giver. Whenever we praise God or give God recognition and acknowledgment, it is for life.

Whenever we give God a spiritual applaud or standing ovation, it is for life. Think about it. God has given us life, something so tremendous, potent, and marvelous that no scholar has ever been smart enough to detail its composition or understand from where it derives its sustaining energy.

Life is a force so complex that it cannot be duplicated. It is, most amazing and thrilling of all. He has given us minds! It is through our minds, the thoughts we think with, and the impressions we store in, that we are conscious of living. In short, your life becomes just what your mind makes it for you and just what it tells you.

On the mind management I have written a very powerful book "**Ageless Mind**" I suggest the reader to kindly read this book very carefully.

In other words, the mind is the author, the principal, the thinker, the planner, the subject as well as the object, behind all our actions. If so, why not discuss about the mind, with the mind, for the mind. The mind that is ageless and requires no rest.

Our mind, which thinks so ceaselessly and insistently, is the most marvelous instrument imaginable; but it is up to us to control it and to choose the kind of thoughts we think, to train ourselves in appreciating all flowers that come into our life, and deal with the weeds.

Yes, we must come to terms with the silent and perennial truth that the field of human life will always consist of the good, the bad and the ugly coexisting together. We all experience the good in our lives, but intertwined with the good is the bad and the ugly. Finding the ugly and unpleasant mixed in with the wheat is an everyday experience and each of us has to deal with the inherent difficulties involved.

Few people go deep enough within their soul to realise in its entire fullness, breadth and scope of the amazing gift of life that enables them to pursue a lifetime of accomplishment. What a marvelous gift. What power! God has endowed us with the power to think, to believe, to create, to imagine, to choose, to feel, to aspire. Having a wonderful sense of appreciation puts all our petty complaints and frustrations, irritants and negativity into perspective.

You live on a realm beyond grudges, ingratitude, selfishness. You enjoy and value each moment and are determined to get the best out of every second.

Do not forget that God is a living energy to quicken and guide our own energy. The Infinite Power source is a living elixir to lift up, sustain, and establish our own spirit.

Being negative takes the spirit out of you. What is the point of God increasing your spirit while you at the same time decrease it with negatives? If you refuse God's gift of an abundant life, then you must do without it.

The most important beginning principle for creating greatness in your life is to recognise and then utilise the principle of personal accountability. Every person comes with the built-in ability to choose their action and reactions for any given set of circumstances.

How we use this ability will ultimately determine all of the outcomes we will experience in our lives. Those who attain the greatest successes in life do so, not because their circumstances have been dramatically different from others, but because their choices have been. It is our personal choices and accountability that have the most significant impact on the kind of lives we propose will lead.

Many people do not realise that even the so-called little moments can have great impact, and it may be easy to justify not giving our attention to them because the consequences may not be immediately apparent. However, an ancient proverb shares this great truth in a different way; "The greatest walls are built with the smallest bricks." Our lives are the same, and we must begin with the little things.

Now, how will you know which little things really deserve your attention? There is an easy solution for us in prioritising all things. Before beginning to sort out life, we need to have a system in place. It is like building a puzzle. In order for the little pieces to be productive and have value we need to understand what the big picture looks like. Our big picture is essentially defining what we want our life to look like, who we want to be and the legacy we want to leave behind.

Many people do not invest the time to answer these important questions. However, if you can do this one step at a time, you will find that all your questions will instantly become clear, and you will be on your path to success. But what is success? The definition is different for every individual, and only you can define your view of success.

Understand that success is a journey and not a destination. It can never be a spot of permanent completion. Success is akin to continual growth. Success is a matter of finding appropriate balance while you are in motion rather than finding a comfortable resting place to stagnate.

Lasting success is found in the balance of four independent elements.

(1) Your feelings about wealth: Success in this area is not based on a specific number on a bank statement. In fact, it has very little to do with money. But it has everything to do with how you feel about what you have. Do you have enough to meet your obligations? To live the life you choose? To be free to pursue the things which are meaningful to you? There are many people who are extremely rich, but not wealthy. How do you feel about your current level of abundance or wealth?

(2) Your feelings about your health: Success has very little to do with quantity of a given thing or an outside measurement. Instead, it has everything to do with the feelings relating to a certain thing. There are many who suffer from disease, disability and challenge who feel very successful in this area. Your feelings about your own health are the important consideration for this issue.

(3) Your feelings about your relationships: "No success can compensate for failure in the home." Everything starts in the home, but relationships also include everyone you interact with. The fullness of success is only enjoyed when we have the ability to share it with another.

(4) Your feelings about your self-achievement, dreams and spirituality: What are your inner most yearnings? What is your connection to things of the spirit? How do you feel about these things? Are your needs being met in this area?

In some ways this area is slightly more important than the others. It is really more of a foundation than a pillar. Until you have these elements being met in your life you cannot inspire or lift another to their greatness. Without this, you are a lot like a lifeguard who can not swim.

When you know who you are and you are confident you are headed in the right direction, magical things happen for you and those around you.

Take a moment right now and stop what you are doing… invest this time in you. Take a careful look at these four areas in your life and consider how satisfied you feel about them.

But lest we become arrogant, we also understand that not only do we live with both the wheat and the thistles but also they exist within each of us. Collectively and individually, we are capable of heart-touching kindness towards one another as well as heartbreaking evil.

We are capable of building up and capable of tearing down, capable of great love and capable of seething hatred, capable of horrendous evil as well as remarkable good.

It will help you to accept life on its own terms rather than struggle against it. Identify and move from the limiting and conflicting, either/or, black or white, all or nothing illusory perception of life to an attitude that is open to all aspects of reality. We do this by accepting life on its own terms. Accepting that pleasure and pain, happiness and unhappiness are all a natural part of the human experience.

When you are able to appreciate life and accept it on

its own terms, you harmonise your mind with God's mind; with the universal intelligence, power and glory. Everyday lift yourself up in your own mind, mood, imagination, and sheer inner conviction. Everyday, give praise to the author of life and glory in its wonders.

Be not afraid of life. Believe that life is worth living and your belief will help create the fact.

15

Health and Happiness are not by Chance

They Have to be Chosen

Are you the happiest person you know, with healthy mind? Not necessarily the lucky, most successful, and, or richest, but just the happiest with healthy mind?

Man's life is incomplete in this world if he has not achieved the quietude and peace of his mind.

If not, why not? Most people will reel off their current worries the job, the kids, the car, the price of food, etc. I don't mean to sweep these aside: problems need to be solved, if you can, or waited out until they disappear. But as far as living happily is concerned you have to face a crucial fact. If you can only live happily after all your problems are solved, you are never going to live happily, because when today's problems are gone and forgotten, others will take their place. So either living happily is just impossible, or you have to do it in spite of your problems.

A quote from the **"BHAGAVAD - GITA"**.

> "I WAS BORNE IN THE DARKEST IGNORANCE, AND MY SPIRITUAL MASTER OPENED MY EYES WITH THE TOUCH OF KNOWLEDGE".

Being happy depends not so much on external circumstances as on your inner life. This means all your thoughts, perceptions, beliefs, emotions, desires, dreams, your entire mental and emotional scene.

Happiness is about how you react inwardly to events, what you think and believe, how you feel, how problems affect you. It may sound obvious, but like many obvious things it is something that is often forgotten when it matters most.

Sanskrit Shloka: -

" Na pranena na apranena martyo jivati Kaschana,
Itarena tu jivanti yasmin etavapasritau."

Meaning : Our life system is not dependant merely on the process of breathing. The intake of diet is indeed important for health, but health does not rest on food alone. The entire system can be thrown out of gear if the mind is upset. A mild turbulence injected into the mind is enough to disturb the entire balance of personality. Your strength is in you.

Religion begins where science ends; the beginning of the higher wisdom.

We focus almost exclusively on our external lives, on getting, spending and having fun, and then wonder why we are not happy. But it is when our inner lives are tranquil that we are happiest and we call this inner peace.

So how is inner peace to be achieved? Is it a question of religion, perhaps, or yoga? These can certainly help but only if they have a positive effect on your inner life. The difficulty is that inner life is based on patterns and habits some you were born with, most you have acquired.

You do not choose, occasion by occasion, how you respond inside when something happens. This happens and you feel angry; that happens you feel sad; you pass the patisserie and you feel hungry; you hear a tune or smell a certain scent and it reminds you of a particular time or a person?

Things produce a response without you thinking about it or choosing how you feel, and they do not necessarily leave you with inner peace.

So the trick is to break the pattern. You can not completely avoid problems, but you can change how you react to them by acquiring new habits that provoke peaceful inner responses.

Training your inner life into different habits requires learning skills of thinking, feeling, and managing your beliefs and desires.

These are very like the virtues many religions and philosophies advocate, but if you think of them as skills rather than virtues, you benefit from an important and liberating shift. Instead of "I must become a better person" you can think "I would live more happily if I worked on my skills".

So the change in attitude becomes a choice, not a duty. And to these remedial skills I have added an extra set of enjoyment skills, otherwise getting happier could turn out a very depressing affair.

This process is not something you can do overnight, it is a whole new way of life, but the reward is what we all want i.e most happiness.

The Greatest Discovery Of Mankind Is That A Human Being Can Change, Alter Or Mould His Life by Altering His Attitude Through His Trained Mind.

The most fortunate happening of my existence is that I have been born as a "Human Being" with superior faculties, to ensure that the human body so awarded, is properly maintained.

The world is like water and the mind of a man like milk. Milk will mix with water if you put the two together. But turn the milk into curd, then churn it and have butter. Now, if you keep the butter in water it will not mix with the water but float unattached. So keep your heart and mind unattached from the materialistic world.

Acquiring all these skills takes time and effort. The important thing is to practice them until they operate without you thinking about them.

Your practice routine will be very individual, because everyone needs to prioritise different skills depending on the specific issues that are holding them back from being happy, but keep the skills in mind and you will constantly find new ways to try them out.

16

Negative Emotions as the Precursor of Disease in the Human Body

The emotions expressed by humans can be divided into two broad categories - Negative or Positive. Negative emotions are for example: apathy, grief, fear, hatred, shame, blame, regret, resentment, anger, hostility. Positive emotions are, for example: interest, enthusiasm, boredom, laughter, empathy, action, and curiosity. Positive and negative emotions are polarities. We can not get rid of one and just keep the other. Ultimately they need to be integrated.

It is also a proven fact that many biochemical and physiological changes occur in our body due to change in our emotional state. Fear, grief, anger each have a characteristic pose and pattern of movement, sometimes referred to as 'Body Language'.

An emotional response, immediately participates contraction of muscles and movement away from structural balance. Once this happens gravity takes over and pulls the structure downwards making the body shorter. Each imbalance must be compensated by displacement of the other parts of the body. Tension and altered functions are always present. Recovery from an emotional shock requires flexibility and resiliency of musculoskeletal system, an ability to return the body towards the ideal pattern of relationship with gravity. If an individual continues to dramatise an emotional situation, the physical body becomes set into a psychological pattern. Once these changes have taken place, the physical attitude becomes invariable, involuntary.

In a balanced body, inspiration involves lengthening of the entire spine, from the sacrum all the way up to the cranium. When individual movements are restricted they can no longer feel an emotion as an emotion. No longer can they have a natural response to an immediate situation and then get on with their life. Instead they live, move and have their being in an attitude. No amount of discussion, thought or mental suggestions can change their pattern. To escape from their chronic fear, grief or anger, the physical tone of the muscles and the structure in relation to gravity must be changed.

The imbalances resulting from physical and emotional trauma can lead to a whole realm of chronic problems for which conventional medicines has little to offer. The more serious of these, arthritis, high blood pressure and even cancer are whole system phenomena that cannot be understood by examining parts rather than relationships. And gravity is a part of whole that has been given relatively little attention.

Tensions may lead to headaches and bursitis. The functioning of the spinal cord itself may be impaired at the important region where it descends from the brain. The electric and magnetic field of the brain and spinal nerves may have their patterns distorted by cervical imbalances.

While physical patterns can become solidified from psychological attitudes, the converse is also true. A physical trauma for e.g. a childhood fall down basement steps, a slip from the bicycle, both as a result of gravity or a devastating motor crash can influence the emotional state. A relatively simple accident, which leaves the body, mal-aligned and out of balance, can affect the psychological sense of individual.

The kinesthetic body feels inadequate and the physical structure projects an image of inadequacy.

Holistic health is the optimal state of wellbeing well physically, emotionally, spiritually and mentally. Wellness is considered to be the state in which the physical, emotional, mental, and spiritual dimensions are balanced so that energy is used effectively. The 'fight or flight' response is the changes in your body that you need if you have to run away from a dangerous situation, a threat to well-being. These changes can create symptoms of anxiety, apprehension, breathlessness, cold sweats, trembling, dilated pupils, nausea or shaking.

Similarly, 'thought' is electrical and cells of the body contain elemental compounds comprising electro-magnetic fields of force. We must remember at all times, our physical body comprising billions of cells, listens continually to our mental demands. If one has thoughts of despair and not wishing to continue one's life and the burden of knowing the named disease, the body will think the same as the cells of the body each have a knowingness, a sort of 'mind of their own' and they will act accordingly.

Biological clocks are mostly set by internal pacemakers, such as thalamus, and that organisms are for the most part, independent of natural energy cycles. It is obvious that life is a part of a larger fabric, and the rhythm of the sun, moon, 9 planets and other celestial bodies much affect us.

Also, 'Chakras' are energy centers associated with bodies. Chakras are rotating vortexes where energy enters and exists. They might have different diameters depending on how much energy is going in and out. Each **chakra relates** to certain qualities and issues. Most commonly, seven chakras are agreed upon, like this: Rootrelates to basic survival and security; Navel-procreation, sex; Solar Plexusfeeling, one's sense of knowing, gut feeling; Heart acceptance and love; Throatone's ability to communicate; Forehead 3rd eye, one's psychic perceptions; Crown spiritual connection to higher levels of awareness. Each of these relate to the ability to deal with issues on a wider scale; the chakras, kind of act as anchor points, forming stable means of interacting with a certain sphere of life.

Western medicine has made astonishing advances in the past two centuries. The fundamental physical mechanism of the body are known and, perhaps, understood. Childbirth, once the primary cause of death in women and children, has been rendered almost routine. The processes of infection and disease transmission have been discovered and controlled. Physicians routinely make astonishing repairs to broken bones, brains, and hearts. A remarkable success has been achieved in countering the acute problems of most peoples' health. But as these acute illnesses and injuries become less prevalent and life-threatening, more chronic problems are emerging: cancer, heart disease, diabetes, mental and spiritual illnesses. It is against these types of challenges that alternative medicine can be used most effectively.

When the life force flows freely throughout the body, a person experiences optimal health and vitality. When the life force is blocked or weakened, organs, tissue, and cells are deprived of the energy they need to function at their full potential, and illness or disease results.

Similarly, 'Healing energy', whether produced by a medical device or projected from the human body, is energy of a particular frequency or set of frequencies that stimulates the repair of one or more tissues.

The curative process is of divergent viewpoints. Conventional medicine promotes the view that external treatments-drugs, surgery, radiation-cure people, and practitioners are trained to fix or repair broken parts. The focus is on the disease process or abnormal conditions.

Alternative practitioners look at conditions that block the life force and keep it from flowing freely through the

seven major chakras of the human body

body. Healing occurs when balance and harmony are restored. The focus is on the health potential of the person rather than the disease problem.

Just as conventional and alternative medicine complement one another, so do multiple perspectives of research. Those who limit themselves to Western scientific research have virtually ignored anything that cannot be perceived by the five senses and repeatedly measured or quantified. Research is dismissed as superstitious and invalid if it cannot be scientifically explained by cause and effect. Many continue to cling with an almost religious fervor to this cultural paradigm about the power of science-more specifically, the power that science gives them. By dismissing non-Western scientific paradigms as inferior at best and inaccurate at worst, the most entrenched members of the conventional medical research community try to counter the threat that alternative therapies and research pose to their work, their well-being, their world views. And yet, biomedical research cannot explain many of the phenomena that concern alternative practitioners regarding caring and healing processes. When therapies such as acupuncture or homeopathy are observed to result in a physiological or clinical response that cannot be explained by the biomedical model, many have tried to deny the results rather than modify the scientific model.

In contrast to the biomedical perspective, Buckminster Fuller, an American architect and inventor, said, "Eighty percent of reality cannot be perceived or detected through the five senses". If researchers limit themselves to the five senses, they will never come to understand human energy fields, electromagnetic fields, thoughts as a form of energy, or the healing power of prayer.

Alternative medicine, however, believes that no single factor causes anything, nor a magic substance single-handedly reverse illness. Multiple factors contribute to illness, and multiple interventions work together to promote healing. The double-blind method is incapable of reconciling this degree of complexity and variation. Although major alternative medical systems may not have a great deal of quantitative research, they are generally not experimental. They rely on well-developed clinical observational skills and experience that is guided by their explanatory models.

In my opinion, Medical science recognizes that many diseases are produced by stress, anxiety, worry and fear. There is an increasing incidence of stress related disease in India like coronary heart disease, cerebro-vascular diseases like cerebral strokes due to hemorrhage in one of the blood vessels in the brain, hypertension, diabetes etc. The only method of preventing the pit falls of these diseases is by way of their early diagnosis and treatment along with a healthy life style of peaceful and blissful living. Please read my book the Art of Blissful Living.

17

Is Stress A Part of Life or It Affects The Body & Mind

Stress is a part of life. But undue stress, unproductive stress or unmitigated stress turns into distress. And, the general feeling is that stress levels have gone up within the last few decades. Let us reflect on how it has happened. During the last few centuries, the world has changed at a pace unprecedented in human history.

Science and technology have given us time-saving gadgets, means of rapid transport, and almost instantaneous communication. However, the more these 'conveniences' have made life easier, the more it seems to have become difficult. The sources of tension in life have not reduced one bit, the world wide web notwithstanding. Human nature has not changed, and therefore hatred, jealousy and intrigues continue to plague mankind as much today as in the days of the Vedic period. Further, the proliferation of consumer goods has made man more self-centred, and increased the frustrations due to unfulfilled (and fulfilled!) desires.

The association between increasing mental stress and the rising prevalence of several diseases of modern civilization has compelled man to sit up and take notice of the time honoured wisdom enshrined in ancient systems such as yoga. While none of these systems can guarantee a life free of stress, they do show a way for acquiring mastery over sources of stress.

Effects of stress on the body and mind

Anyone who has experienced a dry mouth and pounding heart during stress knows that stress affects the body. The effects of stress on the body evolved quite early in the course of evolution, and are primarily designed to help the animal face the stressful situation better. In order to understand how, let us consider an encounter between a lion and a deer. The lion is overcome by an aggressive impulse, and the deer by fear.

These emotions help both animals in intensifying their effort: the lion while it is running to catch the deer, and the deer while it is running to escape. Thus emotional stress intensifies the effort, and improves the chances of success in both the animals. Hence stress is useful. Further, success in the stressful situation depends at least partly on the ability to run well.

The effects of stress on the body help in running better. While running, the exercising muscles need more blood, more oxygen, and more glucose. Increase in heart rate and increase in the force with which the heart beats helps increase blood flow. More blood carries more oxygen to the muscles. Further, the rate and depth of breathing increase, and the airways open up in stress, helping delivery of more oxygen to the body. In stress, glycogen in the liver and muscles also breaks down to release glucose, thereby making more glucose available to the muscles. Several other effects of stress on the body also help. For example, the pupils of the eye become wide open.

As a result, even in dark the animal is able to make the best use of whatever little light is available, and thereby find his way better. In short, stress has effects on the body which are useful in the stressful situation. Hence these effects have survival value.

If the effects of stress on the body are useful, why do they lead to disease in man? To begin with, it needs to be emphasized that they are useful to man as well. Although human beings do not hunt any more, they find it difficult to survive without these mechanisms. But two peculiarities of human life make the same mechanisms harmful under certain conditions.

First, as compared to animals, human beings have a very good memory, and they make plans for the future. As a result, their stress becomes long-term, or chronic. In animals, stress is based only on the present. For example, in the case of a lion chasing a deer, the stress begins when they spot each other, and ends when the deer has been caught, or when it has become out of reach. But in human beings stress may be due to what happened years ago, or what might go wrong years later! Prolonged stress makes some of the effects of acute stress on the body continuous, and that is harmful.

For example, a rise in blood pressure while running is perfectly normal, but it becomes a disease if it is continuous.

Our body, like that of animals, is primarily designed to face acute stress, not for coping up with chronic stress. Secondly, even in acute stress, human beings often do not have to indulge in physical activity. By and large, the 'civilised' man today neither has to chase his prey, nor has to flee from a predator. When he fights with his fellow beings, he generally confines himself to a verbal attack.

Due to absence of physical activity during acute stress, the response may turn harmful. For example, if the muscle and liver glycogen break down to release glucose, but additional glucose does not get utilised because there are no exercising muscles, the glucose remains in blood, thereby raising the blood glucose level.

If prolonged stress makes a high blood glucose level almost continuous, it may contribute to diabetes. Similarly, if the heart beats faster and more forcefully, but the blood flow through muscles does not increase (because muscles are not exercising), the heart will have to work harder, and its hard work will raise the blood pressure even more. If chronic stress makes this rise in blood pressure almost continuous, it may lead to hypertension.

Medical professionals seem to agree that CHRONIC STRESS is one of the biggest killers in the world. Chronic stress means your body is out of balance and your immune system is compromised which allows your body to become a breeding ground for any sickness, anxiety, depression, gastrointestinal disorders, etc. Today the World Health Organization considers that 30% of all buildings are 'sick' buildings.

Technological advances have introduced a wave of harmful building, electronic and decorating materials. Accumulation of chemical vapors, synthetic building material and electromagnetic fields combined with poor ventilation and artificially lighting creates the sick building syndrome. Such hidden chemicals, synthetic material and electromagnetic fields in the home links to diseases like eczema, chronic fatigue syndrome, insomnia, hyperactivity, asthma, etc.

Vastu believes that there are two types of energies in nature, these forces which are equal and opposite in nature. The intersection of these two forces is cosmic ordained and produces a third eye type of force which is called bio-force needed for life to exist. Over the surface of the globe these factors continuously intersect releasing bio-energy. When a structure is built over the surface of the earth it comes in the way of natural intersection.

If the structure is designed as per Vastu principles, the positive forces override the negative forces, which is beneficial to all the inmates to be healthy.

According to law of conservation of energy which is

accepted by scientific community, energy can be neither created nor be destroyed. It can only be changed from one form to another.

It is very important to have synergy between human energy and Earth energy to live life happily. It means one should be very cautious where the house, work place is and the energy is balanced with him to avoid unnecessary troubles. Nowadays, in the whole world, people are aware of Ecology and balancing them with Earth's energies. People are now towards to use natural building materials for healthy living, adopting concepts of Green city and Save Environment. It is also very important to survive from stress, whether it is Geopathic or Electro magnetic stress.

GEOPATHIC STRESS

'Geopathic' literally means 'earth-associated illness. The earth's magnetic field is constantly fluctuating and this causes natural radiation to rise through the ground. This process is helped by deep mine shafts and is intensified by modern deep-ploughing agriculture. The negative forces released are carried by underground streams or take the form of energy lines that can be detected by dowsing. Natural causes of geopathic stress are nowadays compounded by the electromagnetic fields generated by mobile phones, microwaves, cars and so on, which produce stress.

Geopathic Stress is caused by the detrimental effects of negative earth energies which pass through walls, windows, and closed doors. These energies are not stable and can change with the seasons or even with the time of the day and can be distorted by building works carried out even at some distance away.

Geopathic stress is a form of trauma caused by disturbed or anomalous energies within the earth's mantle. The earth is surrounded by an energy grid which contains and transmits vital forces. This grid is essential for life and is a part of the background radiation which supports life.

Within the earth there is naturally occurring beneficial radiation but when the earth is disturbed, e.g. by digging, including building and construction work or due to any natural disasters such as earthquakes, landslide, this balance can be altered and the harmful energies can be released underneath the ground surface. Geopathic stress therefore represents a distortion of the natural frequency which can sometimes be observed visibly in nature-Eggplants failing to thrive, trees taking on peculiar angles and trunk developments. In contrast some plants seem to positively flourish in areas where geopathic stress has been detected.

Researchers and scientists have noted that Geopathic Stress does not necessarily cause illness but seems to lower a person's immune system, so if they are sleeping in an area that is geopathically stressed, their body is not getting a proper chance to repair. In recent years the rapid proliferation of artificial sources of radio electric frequencies has become a cause for concern. It has surpassed many times the production of natural sources.

It is interesting that where Geopathic stress has been found, the occupants of that property have often noted that since moving there, their health has deteriorated, their sleep has not been restful and previously happy families are encountering more arguments or a sense of unhappiness. It has also been found that houses where geopathic stress is found are often harder to sell and return to the market regularly as people have not been comfortable there. Positive relationships with neighbours may have also suffered. Geopathic stress in the work place also seems to generate its own tensions with a work force who can be argumentative and un-cooperative, or who may not stay in the job long or there is a higher incidence of sick leave.

Nowadays, there is a tendency for people to talk of 'energies', 'fields', 'ley lines', 'telluric energy', 'subtle energies' and so on. Very often these names are interchangeable. But there is little agreement about what the words mean. Usually an electromagnetic quality which can be sensed intuitively is acknowledged. No wonder that traditional science, which can only accept the existence of something they can 'prove' of, is slow to embrace this world of uncertainty.

Common symptoms of geopathic stress can include: fatigue, weak immune system, depression, and nervousness, loss of appetite, poor digestion, allergies, insomnia, circulation problems, muscle cramps, and grinding of teeth. Children are especially sensitive to geopathic stress. Bed wetting and continuous crying by babies may occur.

Fortunately, there are ways in which we can identify and neutralize many forms of geopathic stress. Electronic instruments can be used to measure electromagnetic fields, microwave radiation, poisonous gases, and radioactivity. Dowsing can be used to identify the more subtle energy fields. After we identify the cause and the location of the geopathic stress, we can rectify the soil. By stimulating the energy channels and energy centers of the Earth using copper tubes, natural quartz crystals, and other specially designed tools, can transform the energetic blueprint in a home or property, resulting in tangible and significant health benefits. Most types of geopathic stress can be substantially reduced, or in some cases entirely eliminated, using these special techniques and tools. In areas of extremely heavy geopathic stress, however, relocation to a new place might be the only real solution.

Effect of Orientation on Brain Functioning

Recent research in modern science has now confirmed that our brain is highly sensitive to orientation, position, and direction in space.

The obvious conclusion is that one's inherent sense of direction (orientation) and order gets confused in daily life when one lives in a building with wrong orientation, not build according to Vedic Architecture and Vastu Principle resulting in physiological, psychological, and behavioral imbalances of all kinds.

In Vastu, direction is very important as well as the position and placement of various rooms are taken care of while constructing houses. I have observed that if the people using the South entrances and West entrances of their homes and offices are having a harder time in life, compared to people with North and East entrances. One can observe that even animals and birds (pigeon) are aware of the knowledge of directions. Flowers (sunflower especially) turn to the sun, birds building their nest facing certain directions.

Studies suggest that birds orientate themselves to the compass points using the position of the sun during the day, and the stars at night. They can also sense magnetic north. In addition they use other clues such as visual layout of the land, smell (of the sea), sound (waves on shores, winds through mountain passes). The most amazing aspect of bird migration is that the location, route and perhaps even the techniques are hard wired into their brains. Many migrating birds abandon their young as soon as they fledge, and a short time later, the young make the migration on their own.

Of utmost importance is the orientation of the structure with respect to the cardinal points of the compass.

According to Vastu Science, please refer to my earlier book title **Vastu Science for 21st Century, to enjoy the gift of nature**, a network of energy lines covers the globe of the Earth: an energy grid. These lines are very similar to what we know as the longitude and latitude lines. The lines are conduits by which the energy concentrated at the center of the vital Earth flows out and spreads over the Earth. They are also lines of absorption of solar, lunar and stellar energies. The Earth pulsates with life and rays its energy through this grid system. Vastu Science relates that all planets are suspended or soaked in the ocean of space, which is the source of energy that sustains all embodied energies including man and other animate beings that live on the Earth.

Since the Earth spins from west to east and North Pole is inclines by 23.5 degree, the actual North point of the earth is situated at North East and South point at South West. The cosmic energy coming from North East provides positive energy to the structures where as South West gives rise to negative energy; hence efforts must be made to conserve the positive energy coming from North East and also to arrest the flow of negative energy arising from South West. This is exactly the scientific reason why we keep maximum open spaces and doors in North East of the plot and the least in the South West.

In order to maintain uninterrupted flow in the Earth's magnetic field, it is essential that NO pillars are erected in the middle part of the building and the numbers of windows in the North are double of the South, thus ensuring maximum utilization of positive magnetic flow.. Earth is a Magnet; it has a North Pole and a South Pole. The surface of the earth has magnetic grids called Hartman grids.

These energies represent quality of form and it is the ground on which water, fire, and air can function. We are influenced by geomagneting energy and cosmic energy-The geomagnetic energies vibrates at various frequencies-these energies flows through our building and environment influence us.

We can measure human energy by cosmic global and telluric energy using lecher antena at the frequency level cosmic energy-12 lambda, Global energy- 15.3 lambdas, and telluric energy 8 lambdas. It gives the direction towards our energy levels and shows mental imbalance, physics disorder emotional values or sensational values like smell, movements, feelings etc.

The evidence of rapidly accumulating the electric and electromagnetic fields can cause our mental, emotional and physical health. It is recognized now that some frequencies like X rays and ultra violet rays are harmful but we must think over the domestic and office appliances, overhead and underground high voltage cables, mobile phones and their controversial masts, satellite and communications dishes broadcasting at microwave frequencies and latest wireless Wi-Fi technology. More and more people are reporting electrical sensitivity which is recognized as a medical condition.

Our body has its own electrical system. Electrical energy created in the brain regulates complex biological process. Our bodies electrics can be distributed and disrupted by environmental electromagnetic fields, natural (geo pathos stress) and man made (electro stress) and the effects are the same.

Geopathic stress suppresses immune function. Any natural weaknesses or genetic disorders are amplified. Most significant consistent effect of electro stress on the human system is on the body's ability to absorb nutrients. Every client whose body is detrimentally affected by electro magnetic disturbances has a compressed nutrient absorption rate. Once the source of electro magnetic disturbances is deactivated or removed, nutrient absorption rate rapidly returns to optimal levels.

Electro magnetic fields are invisible to the naked eye, but it shows harmful effect on our body. So electromagnetic field have been part of the earth's environment. Resonances occurs between the earth's molten iron nickel core and the charged gases of the ionosphere. These pulses at definite frequencies (between 0.1 and 25 HZ mostly at about 10 Hz) and act as regulators for the biological time clocks of all living creatures. If a man or any living animal or plant is shielded from these fields for any length of time the result is discomfort, disorientation and even death.

Anything which uses electricity for its operation generates a field, whether it is AC or DC. Automotive currents are in general more harmful because they pulse. In most crystal digital wrist watches, they use automating current to drive or display. So just imagine, wearing a fancy watch on your wrist- can be a stress generator!!!

Due to geopathic stress and environment stress there can be impact on our life. Our body has an energy axis which is aligned with the centre of the body, when it is resonates with the flow of energies in the space. When disturbed, the axis moves, out and causes loss of immunity and health disorders over a period of time. The human body cell has a wave length of 20 cm. All radiations having wavelengths less than 20 cm and therefore a higher vibratory frequency than the Human cell affect the body either positively or negatively.

Almost all radiations, known to mankind have a wavelength of less than 20 cm. All these technologies have made our life easier. Modern society is inconceivable without computers, television and radio. Mobile phones have greatly enhanced the ability of individuals to communicate with each other. Scientific reports have suggested that exposure to electromagnetic fields emitted from these devices could have adverse health effects, such as cancer, reduced fertility, memory loss, and adverse changes in the behavior and development of children.

The above discussion makes it clear that prolonged stress can act through various mechanisms to increase the risk of high blood pressure, heart disease, diabetes, peptic ulcer, infections, cancer, allergies and autoimmune diseases.

Stress being such a common phenomenon, that is a very depressing thought indeed!

A bright implication of these facts, however, is that the reverse of stress, i.e. positive emotions, can do just the opposite. Not only can positive emotions prevent illness, they can even heal an illness. In other words, the disease process initiated by stress is reversible.

One can realize that if stress could make him sick, cheerfulness might make him well again. He treated himself with laughter, by watching comedies in the company of good joyful friends, and actually recovered.

The key to stress management is to develop a clear insight into the problem. To get the insight, it is helpful to ask oneself a few searching questions. Find a quiet corner, relax, and ask yourself these questions during meditation. The sooner you do so, the better, because the more you let stress accumulate, the more difficult the issue might get.

1. What is the stress due to?

Think dispassionately and try to identify the cause of stress. Is it an illness? Is it an unpleasant job? Is it marital disharmony? Is it a delinquent child? Is it a financial problem? Is it litigation?

2. Does it really matter?

Ask yourself whether you really have a major problem on head, or is it merely an inconvenience.

If you think there is nothing that can be done about the problem, do at least one thing: relax!

We cannot change others but we can change ourselves. We can look at circumstances differently, and that can take all the misery away although the circumstances remain exactly the same. Look at our circumstances as we choose is the ultimate freedom which nobody can take away from us.

Specific measures for stress relief

- About twenty minutes of meditation, preferably twice a day, is very relaxing, and has a carry over effect during the rest of the day.
- Work is an excellent emotional anaesthetic. If you keep yourself busy with work, or hobbies, and get absorbed in them, you will have little time to worry. On the other hand, an idle mind tends to brood over problems, which in turn aggravates stress.
- Try to find someone else whom you can help someone with a worry, someone who is sick, children whom you can teach, or a philanthropic organization in need of volunteers. Apart from being good in itself, such activities relieve stress in several ways. First, you realize that you are not the only one with problems, and that makes you feel better. Secondly, you may find that your problems are very small as compared to other people's problems. A person stops complaining about not having shoes when he finds a person not having feet. Finally, getting involved in someone's problems reduces our absorption.
- Find a way of expressing your feelings. For example, you may start writing a diary. If you are more creative, you may find self- expression in writing poetry or in painting.
- Talking our problems over with someone makes us feel lighter. We may also get some good advice, but what we need most is someone to listen to you. However, we cannot open ourselves to everyone. The person in whom we confide should have the following qualities:
  - He should be your well wisher.
  - He should have empathy, or at least sympathy.
  - He should be a good listener.
  - He should have the time to listen, and should be willing to spare the time.
  - He should be able to keep secrets.
  - He should be wise enough to give good advice.

If you have one such person in your life, you are indeed lucky. If you do not have even one such person in life, you are indeed lucky. If you do not have even one such person in life, there is nothing to feel bad about: you have plenty of company. If you do not have a friend or relative to confide in, consult a doctor, preferably a psychiatrist, or a counselor. These are good supports. Their relationship with us is professional rather than emotional, and they may charge us for their time.

However, there is one support having all the desirable qualities in a confidante plus more: God. He is always available to all of us. We can share all our problems with Him, and receive His guidance in the form of our inner voice. He loves us, and has all the time to listen to us. If we find it difficult to relate to a nameless, formless God, we can relate to His human forms an avatar, prophet, guru anyone in whom we have faith, and with whom we have established a bond.

To recognize His voice, we need receptivity and complete sincerity anything which smacks of egoism, selfishness or hatred cannot be His voice. He loves all of us, and therefore His voice is based on unqualified love even for our opponents. Moreover, following only His voice can bring us lasting inner peace and happiness.

Yantra

Yantra is a symbolic representation of mantras. They are emblems of psychic powers.Yantras are made of metals, gemstones, alloys etc.Yantra literally means "Loom, Instrument or Machine". In actual practice, a Yantra is a symbolic representation of aspects of divinity, usually the Mother Goddess. It is an interlocking matrix of geometric.

Figures, circles, triangles and floral patterns that form fractal patterns of elegance and beauty. Vedic Yantra is geometrical figures intended to represent the basic energies. Just as every elementary geometrical figure, a straight line, a square, a cross or a triangle etc., has a symbolic value corresponding to the basic notions, similarly, the Yantra symbolize one or the other power or energy. Yantra can be drawn, engraved or painted on a variety of substances. The classical eight surfaces are gold, silver, copper, crystal, birch, bone, hide (which can include any type of paper), and Vishnu stone (shaligrama).

Everything in the universe is made of energy. The cosmos is the biggest source of energy and the planets are the biggest bodies that cause the energy disturbance. If you are doing something that means you are attracting a certain type of energy. But if you are getting difficulties in something it means that you are not attracting the like energies. In our ancient Indian Vedic science, there are some special sound's vibrations to control and concentrate these Cosmic Energies, we called them Mantras, and the geometrical shapes of these Mantras (special sounds) are called Yantra.

One can change the negative energy to positive energy through vedic mantra and yantra. Please refer my preview book: **A Practical Guide to an Ageless Mind.**

18

Conclusion

The human race in the 21st Century is encountering changes at a tremendous speed. A number of opportunities as well as challenges are lying in the lap of the future and unless we gear up to face those challenges to grab those opportunities within a proper time frame we are in for a massive adaptation breakdown.

The social stresses which will be generated by the developmental forces might lead to the total collapse of human civilization and we will be doomed if we do not prepare for them accordingly.

On the contrary, proper channelization of these forces and suitable adjustment in our values will make life much more easier, much more comfortable a life really worth living, but one must know the art of living with the help of Vedic Knowledge - the gift of nature.

Your strength is within you. Religion begins where science ends and marks the beginning of the higher wisdom.

Before I close, let us chant together a Vedic prayer from the Upanishad.

The meaning of the prayer is:

O Lord, lead me from the unreal to the ultimate reality, from the darkness to light, and from the death of ignorance to the immortality of knowledge.

Sanskrit Shloka :

Serve Bhavantu Sukhinah
Serve Santu Niramaya,

Serve Bhadrani Pashyantu
Ma Kaschid dukhbhagbhavet.

Aum asaoto maa sadgamaya
Tamaso maa jyotirgamaya

Mruytorma amrutam gamaya
Aum Shantih ! Shantih !! Shantih !!!

Book Reviews

This book explains in simple prose the cycle of life, causes of mental tension, its remedies, positive and negative emotions of the human beings. The highly erudite author conveys the true message that "we are spirits eternally free birth less and deathless". So we should not worry too much about death. Live a joyous and tension free life by leaving everything to the Almighty.

Prof. P. K. Arya
Chairman, Media Trust of India.

As a Medical Practitioner I can say it with authority that stress is the root cause of most the psychosomatic diseases. The stress arises due to various imaginary reasons which can be avoided if a person adopts the simple methods mentioned in this book. I highly recommend this book to all who wants to lead a tension free life and more particularly to those people who are in a hurry to achieve more. The author's simple advice to them is live with the nature and there should be harmony between the mind and body.

Padmabhushan Dr. S. K. Sama
Former Chairman, Board of Governors,
Sir Ganga Ram Hospital, New Delhi.

After reading this book I came to the conclusion that it is wiser to live in the present. We cannot lead a peaceful life if we worry too much about the future. Therefore, I simply agree with the learned author of this excellent book

Let us live in the present and make proper use of it without any mental tension.

Dr P S Rana

Former Chairman and M.D.

HUDCO, New Delhi.

This book explains in detail how to bring purity in our life by avoiding negative energies and hatred for others. One should not worry too much about death because soul is eternal. In order to have a peaceful life a person should first of all liberate his mind from negative thoughts. His actions should be useful to him, to the society and to the nation. The highly respected author of this book vividly narrates the insights on how to lead a positive life.

Howard Beckman

Director

Vedic Cultural Fellowship, New Mexico U.S.A.

I read this book and find that it contains valuable inputs which will help a person to lead a purposeful and peaceful life. It advocates the need for living according to the principles of nature and also the need for change in our attitude towards others. In short, a very useful book for all, for the scholar as well as for a layman.

Muraleedharan Nair

This Latest book of Prof Dr B B Puri, perfectly describes that "whenever you open this book of knowledge, you will receive benefits". The work of an evolved master. The distilled wisdom flows through every line and pages.

Raman Mehta

NOTES

NOTES

NOTES

NOTES

NOTES

NOTES

NOTES

NOTES

NOTES

NOTES